1997

Arden's Housing Library

8.

The Series Editors of Arden's Housing Library
are **Andrew Arden QC** and **Caroline Hunter**.
The team of expert authors is drawn from the
members of Arden Chambers and other
practitioners.

Arden's Housing Library provides accessible
guidance to the details of housing rights and
duties for those involved in the management of
social housing. It breaks up the whole subject into
digestible segments and approaches each topic
from the perspective of its practical application.
Information about other titles in the Library is
given at the back of this book.

Josephine Henderson is a practising barrister at Arden Chambers in London, specialising in housing, landlord and tenant, and local government law.

Rights to Buy and Acquire

Law and Practice
in the Management
of Social Housing

Josephine Henderson, Barrister

First published in Great Britain 1997 by
Lemos & Crane
20 Pond Square
Highgate
London N6 6BA.
Telephone 0181-348 8263

ISBN 1-898001-19-7

A CIP catalogue record for this book is available from
the British Library

Design by Mick Keates
Typset by Concise Artisans, London
Printed by Redwood Books, Trowbridge

Contents

Table of Cases   xi
Table of Statutes   xiv
Table of Statutory Instruments   xix

Introduction   1

1. Who has the Right to Buy?   5
    Secure tenants   5
        Requirements of a secure tenancy   5
        Tenancies that are not secure   7
        Loss of security   10
    Joint tenants   12
        Loss of right by a joint tenant   12
    Family members   13
        Who is a family member?   13
        Occupying requirements   14

2. Qualifications and Exceptions   16
    The qualifying period   16
        Relevant periods   17
        Public sector tenant   21
    Exceptions to right to buy   22
        Excepted landlords   22
        Insufficient interest in property 23
        Excepted property   23

3. What is Bought?   29
    The dwelling-house   29
    House or flat   30
        The reasonable test   31
        Horizontal division   31
        Vertical division   31

Material part over remainder of structure 32
Interest to be conveyed or granted 33
  Length of lease 33
  Exception for blocks of flats 33

4. Procedure 34
Service of notices 35
  Place of service 35
Mistakes in notices 36
Basic procedure 37
Landlord's costs 37
Tenant's notice 38
  Family members 38
  Extended right to buy 38
Landlord's reply 38
  Landlord's acceptance or denial 39
  Landlord's offer notice 39
Tenant's notice of intention 42
  Proceeding with the claim 42
  Withdrawing the claim 43
  Seeking rent to mortgage terms 43
Completion 43
  Status of other occupiers on completion 44
Registration of title 44
Dealing with procedural delays 45
  Delay by tenant 45
  Delay by landlord 49

5.   **The Price and Paying It** 53
Value of dwelling-house 53
  Who should conduct the valuation? 53
  Valuation assumptions 54
  Reduction for operative notice of delay 57
Disputes about valuation 57
  Determination 58
  Re-determination 58
  Procedure by district valuer 59
  Challenging the district valuer 59

Procedure following determination 59
The discount 60
Percentage entitlement 60
Entitlement to discount 61
Change of tenant 63
Paying for the property 63
Right to acquire on rent to mortgage terms 63
Persons entitled to the scheme 64
When the right cannot be exercise 64
Procedure 67
Terms in conveyance or grant 72
Redemption of landlord's share 74

6. **The Grant or Conveyance** 76
Repayment of discount 76
Relevant disposals 77
Exempt disposals 78
Amount to be repaid 78
Charge on the property 79
Covenants common to leasehold and freehold interests 81
Rights to be conveyed or granted 81
Related rights 81
Restrictive covenants 82
Other covenants and conditions 82
Covenants to be included in freehold conveyances 83
Nature of interest 83
Covenants to be included in grant of a lease 84
Nature of interest 84
Rights to be included 84
Covenants by landlord to repair and maintain 84
Covenants by tenant 86
Provisions affecting future disposals 91
Agreements in superior leases 91
Limitations on future disposals by tenants in
National Parks 91

7. **Loss and Enforcement of Right to Buy** 93
Circumstances where right to buy may be lost 93

	Loss of security	93
	Ineligibility for right to buy	98
	Change of tenant	101
	Withdrawal and lapse of right to buy	102
	Withdrawal and deemed withdrawal by tenant	102
	Withdrawal by landlord	102
	Enforcement and resolution of disputes	103
	Injunctions and declarations	103
	Judicial review	106
	Intervention of Secretary of State	107
8.	**Changes in the Landlord's Interest**	112
	Right to buy was (or was about to be) admitted	
	before landlord's disposal of property	112
	Landlord condition satisfied	112
	Landlord condition not satisfied	113
	Right to buy already (or about to be) denied	113
	Landlord condition satisfied	113
	Landlord condition not satisfied	114
	Completion already taken place	114
	Preservation of right to buy	114
	Qualification for preserved right	115
	Exceptions to preserved right	115
	Qualifying persons	115
	The preserved rights	116
	Moves by the tenant	117
	Disposal of landlord's interest	118
	Further disposals of landlord's interest	119
	Extended right to buy	120
9.	**Extension of Right**	121
	Legislation	121
	When does extended right apply?	122
	Modifications of right to buy	122
	Procedure	123
	Claiming the right to buy	123
	Admitting or denying the right	123
	Withdrawal of tenant's notice	123

Notice of offer	124
Change of landlord or tenant	124
Apportionment of purchase price	125
Execution of conveyance	125
Right to acquire on rent to mortgage terms	126
Claiming the right	126
Admitting or denying the right	126
Withdrawal of notice	126
Change of landlord	127
Apportionment of initial payment	127
Execution of conveyance	127
Redemption of freeholder's share	128
Tenant's notice of delay	128
Registration of title	128
Repayment of discount	129
Secretary of State's power to intervene	129
Assistance to freeholder	129
Inclusion of land	130
Covenants in the conveyance	130
10. Housing Associations and Other Registered Social Landlords	**131**
Housing associations within the right to buy	132
Calculating the qualifying period	132
Who has the right to buy?	132
Covenants in conveyance or lease (National Parks, etc)	132
Financial arrangements	132
Housing associations outside the right to buy	133
Associations excluded from right	134
Leasehold schemes for the elderly	135
Tenants' incentive scheme	136
The scheme	136
Eligibility	136
Procedure	137
Right to acquire under Housing Act 1996	137
Registered social landlord	137
Who has the right to acquire?	138

Procedure and price   140
Consultation   141
Voluntary sales   141

Index   143

Table of Cases

Barwick and Barwick v Kent County Council
(1992) 24 HLR 341..24–5

Blake v Barking and Dagenham London Borough Council
(1996) *The Times*, 11 November...42, 54

Boswell v Crucible Steel Co of America [1925] 1 KB 119................41

Bradford City Metropolitan Council v McMahon
(1993) 25 HLR 534..43, 95, 97

Bristol City Council v Lovell (1996) 29 HLR....................................105

Burrows v Brent London Borough Council
(1996) 29 HLR 167, HL...99

Campbell v City of Edinburgh District Council 1987 SLT 51.....9–10

Coventry City Council v Cole (1993) 25 HLR 555, CA....................89

Crawley Borough Council v Sawyer (1987) 20 HLR 98......................6

Dance v Welwyn Hatfield District Council [1990] 1 WLR 1097...104

Dickinson v Enfield London Borough Council
(1996) 29 HLR 465, CA...55

Dyer v Dorset County Council [1989] QB 346...................................24

Elvidge v Coventry City Council (1993) 26 HLR 281, CA...............11

Enfield London Borough Council v McKeon
[1986] 1 WLR 1007, CA...100

Freeman v Wanbeck District Council [1984] 2 All ER 746..............26

Greenfield v Berkshire County Council (1996) 28 HLR 691...........10

Greenwich London Borough Council v Regan
(1996) 28 HLR 469, CA...99

Guinan v Enfield London Borough Council
(1996) 29 HLR 456, CA...51, 83

3

Hamilton v City of Glasgow District Council
1996 SLT (Lands Tr) 14..20

Harrogate Borough Council v Simpson (1984) 17 HLR 205............14

Harrow London Borough Council v Tonge
(1992) 25 HLR 99..14, 95

Heinemann v Cooper (1987) 19 HLR 262..89

Hounslow London Borough Council v Hare *et al*
(1990) 24 HLR 9..134

Hughes v Greenwich London Borough Council
[1993] 3 WLR 821; (1994) 26 HLR 99..9

Hussey v London Borough of Camden (1994) 27 HLR 5, CA........10

James v Mansfield District Council
(28 October 1988, unreported), CA..103

Jennings and Jennings v Epping Forest District Council
(1992) 25 HLR 241..94

Maltglade v St Albans Rural District Council
[1972] 2 All ER 129..35

McIntyre v Merthyr Tydfil District Council
(1989) 21 HLR 320, CA..63, 101

Milius's Application, *Re* (1995) 70 P&CR 427................................92

Milne-Berry and Malden v Tower Hamlets London
Borough Council (1995) 28 HLR 225................................36, 49

Muir Group Housing Association v Thornley
(1992) 25 HLR 89..94–6

Pearlman v Harrow School [1979] 1 All ER 356................................41

R v Council of the City of Plymouth and Cornwall County
Council, *ex p* John Charles Freeman (1986) 18 HLR 243..........23, 106

R v Secretary of State for the Environment, *ex p* Norwich City
Council [1982] QB 808; [1982] 1 All ER 737, CA................54, 108, 110

R v Secretary of State for the Environment, *ex p* West
Oxfordshire District Council (1993) 26 HLR 417................................28

Sharpe v Duke Street Securities (1987) 19 HLR 506..........................31

South Glamorgan County Council v Griffiths
(1992) 24 HLR 334...9

Sutton London Borough Council v Swann
(1985) 18 HLR 140...95–6, 102

Taylor v Newham London Borough Council
[1993] 1 WLR 444, CA..105

Wood v South Western Co-operative Housing
Society 91982) 4 HLR 101..135

Table of Statutes

Charities Act 1960.................134
Children Act 1989..................12
Companies Act 1985.............138
Family Law Act 1996...12, 99, 115
  s 30(4)..........................6
Housing Act 1974
  s 31...........................135
Housing Act 1980......... 1, 36, 54
Housing Act 1985................1, 36
  Part II..........................24
  Part III..........................7
  Part IV..........................6
  Part V.....................37, 140
  Part VII..........................7
  s 5, (2)........................134
  s 6............................ 134
  s 27B............................7
  s 30....................... 113, 119
  s 79(3)..........................6
  s 80..................6-8, 114, 118
  s 81............................6
  s 86...........................101
  s 87..................15, 95, 97
  s 89(2)..........................95
  s 91...........................101
  s 92...................56, 101
  s 93(2)................. 10, 94
  s 112............................5
  s 115...................21, 138
  s 118...................29, 93
    (1).............................5
    (2)...........................12
  s 119 16
  s 120 22
  s 121 ....65, 98, 100

    (1)............................98
    (2)...........................100
  s 122 ....13, 15, 37-9, 71,
    ....102, 123, 126
    (3)..............38, 102, 123
  s 122A...........................123
  s 123.................. 13, 38, 62, 95
    (3)...........................13
  s 124.............27, 37, 39, 49-51,
    ....114, 123-4
    (1)(b)..........................39
  s 124A...........................123
  s 125......30, 37, 40-2, 47, 49-51,
    ...... 56, 58, 60, 88-90, 101,
    ....105, 125
    (4A)...........................40
  ss 125A-125C.....................89
  s 125D............... 37, 40, 42, 101
    (2)...........................45-6
  s 125E.................. 42, 46, 102
    (1)...........................40
    (2), (3).......................46
    (4)..........................40, 46
  s 126..............................53, 66
  s 127..............................53-4
    (1)(b).........................55
    (c)............................56
    (4)............................55
  s 128...........................40, 57
    (2), (3)........................58
    (4)............................59
    (5)................42, 59, 101
  s 129, (2)..............................60
  s 130...............................62
  s 131..............................61, 75

s 136..... 63, 95, 101–2, 124, 127
  (1)...........................105
  (2)............................40
s 137........................ 39, 71, 124
  (1)...........................113
  (2).......................113–14
s 138............ 39, 43, 96, 99, 100
  (1).........................104–5
  (2).........................43, 48
  (3)...................43, 104–5
s 138A...............................125
s 139.............................70, 76
  (1A)...........................125
  (2).......................44, 125
s 140..................... 40, 47–8, 71
  (4)............................47
s 141....................... 48, 71, 102
  (1), (2), (4).................40
s 143...........................41, 116
s 143B............................ 65
s 144............ 43, 48, 64, 67, 126
  (2)............................71
  (4)...........................126
a 144A............................ 126
s 146..... 47, 66–7, 69–70, 126–7
s 146B............................ 70–1
s 147.............................69
s 148 ....62, 68
s 149........................71, 127
s 150.......................70, 129
  (2)............................70
ss 150A, 150B..................... 127
s 151 72
  (1A)..................... 127–8
  (2)........................... 128
s 151B.......................69, 72, 80
  (8), (9)......................70

ss 152, 153............................71
s 153A................... 50, 71, 128
  (3), (6)........................50
s 153B.......................51–2, 128
  (1)............................ 57
s 154 .... 44, 114
  (2)............................ 44
  (3)............................ 45
  (5A)........................ 128
s 155................60, 77, 96, 116
  (2)............................ 77
  (3)................ 72, 77, 79
s 156 ....72, 79, 81
  (2A), (2B), (4A)......... 80
s 156A...............................129
s 157.................................117
s 159................................73, 77
s 160.................................78
s 163.................................91
s 164...... 59, 106–7, 117, 129, 140
  (2)...........................107
  (5A)......................... 129
s 165.....................109, 117, 140
s 166...... 107, 109, 117, 129, 140
s 166A...........................129, 140
ss 167, 168...........109, 117, 140
s 169.............107, 109, 117, 140
s 170.....................110, 117, 140
s 171.................................121
s 171A......................113–15
s 171B(2)............................115
  (6)............................117
s 171D, (2)...........................119
s 171E(1)..............................120
s 171F.................................118
s 171G...............................117
s 171H.................................113

s 176.....................34, 117
    (2)..............................38
    (3)..............................35
    (4)..............................36
s 177...............................103
    (2)..............................36
s 177A.............................125
s 178................................37
s 179................................91
    (1)..............................22
s 180................................39
s 181...... 30–1, 39, 58, 103, 109
s 183............................29–31
    (2)(a)–(c)....................32
s 184.........................30, 78, 130
    (4)..............................30
s 186................................14
s 187.........................21, 138
s 621A..............................88
Sched 1.....................6, 8, 10
    para 2..........................11
Sched 2
    ground 9.....................118
    ground 16...................100
Sched 4.........................16, 60
    para 5..........................24
    para 6.............16, 21, 25
    para 7..........................21
    paras 8, 9....................21
    para 10........................26
    para 11........................27
Sched 5............9, 22–3, 112–13,
    ....119, 132
    para 1........115, 122, 140
    para 2........115, 122, 134
    para 3 115, 122, 135, 140
    para 4....................23, 44

para 11.....................140
Sched 5A..........................117
Sched 6..............................72
    Part I....................76, 81
    Parts II, III............76, 84
    paras 2, 3...................82
    para 4A.....................130
    para 5...........82–3, 87–9
    para 6........................82
    para 9........................33
    para 11......................84
    para 12.................33, 44
    (3)....................44, 117
    para 13......................84
    para 14(2).................84
    (c).........................88
    (3)..............................85
    (4)..............................86
    para 16......................86
    para 16A.................86–7
    para 16B.................86–9
    (2), (3)(a)................89
    (4)..............................88
    para 16C..........86–8, 90
    para 16D...................86
    para 16E............86–7, 91
    para 17......................91
    para 18......................88
    para 19......................91
    para 21A...................130
Sched 6A 72, 128
    para 1(2)...................73
    para 2........................73
    para 4........................75
    para 5.................75, 109
    para 6........................73
    para 7........................75

para 7A......................128
para 8...........................75
paras 9, 10..................74
para 12........................75
Sched 9A 117, 119
para 6........................ 119
para 7(1) (2)..............117
(3)......................119
Housing Act 1988..............7, 131
s 50....................................135–6
s 51...135
ss 52, 53................................136

Housing Act 1996.....1, 4, 131–41
Part I, Chap III....................139
s 1.. 137
s 2.. 137
(2), (4).............................138
s 5.. 138
s 8.. 141
s 11................................133, 141
ss 12–15................................141
s 16.......................................137
(2), (3)........................139
s 17................................137, 140
(1)(a), (b)..................141
ss 18, 25................................139

Housing and Planning
Act 1986................................... 1
s 4(4)................................... 86

Housing Associations Act 1985
ss 8, 9............................133, 141
s 12......................................141
s 41......................................135
s 55 135
s 58(2)..................................135
Sched 1, para 2...................135

Housing Finance Act 1972....135

Income and Incorporation Taxes
Act 1988
s 367(5)............................... 67

Industrial and Provident
Societies Act 1965...134, 137–8

Landlord and Tenant Act 1954
Part II... 8

Landlord and Tenant Act 1985
s 11...90

Land Registration Act 1925
s 8...44
s 14(1)......................................44
s 22..44
s 123...44

Law of Property Act 1925
s 19, (2)....................................14
s 34...13
s 35...14
s 62...81
s 84(1)(aa)................................92
s 139...44

Leasehold Reform Act 1967....31

Leasehold Reform, Housing
and Urban Development
Act 1993............................ 1, 27
s 108......................................63
s 137(2)...............................90

Local Government Act 1972
ss 231, 233.............................36

Local Government
(Miscellaneous Provisions)
Act 1982
s 33.......................................83

Matrimonial Causes
  Act 1973.................................. 12

Matrimonial Homes
  Act 1983........................... 12, 99
    s 1....................................... 115
      (6).................................... 6

Mental Health Act 1983.......... 26

Settled Land Act 1925
  s 39..141

Trustee Act 1925
  s 34..13

Table of Statutory Instruments, Declarations and Determinations

Statutory Instruments

Housing (Extension of Right to Buy) Order 1987............................ 23
    para 3(2).. 23
Housing (Extension of Right to Buy) Order 1993
    (SI No 2240)...121–2, 124, 126–8, 130
Housing (Preservation of the Right to Buy)
    Regulations (SI No 2241).. 116
    Sched 2..116
Housing (Right to Acquire) Regulations 1997 (SI No 619)........... 140
Housing (Right to Acquire) (Discount) Order 1997 (SI No 626)..141
Housing (Right to Acquire) (Discount) (Wales) Order 1997
    (SI No 569).. 141
Housing (Right to Buy Delay Procedure) (Prescribed Forms)
    Regulations 1989 (SI No 240)...34
Housing (Right to Buy) (Maximum Discount) Order
    1989 (SI No 513)... 61
Housing (Right to Buy) (Prescribed Forms) Regulations
    1994 (SI No 2194)..34, 67
Housing (Right to Buy) (Prescribed Forms) (Welsh Forms)
    Regulations 1994 (SI No 2931)...34
Housing (Right to Buy) (Prescribed Persons) Order
    1992 (SI No 1703).. 22
Housing (Right to Buy) (Service Charges) Order 1986
    para 3..89
    para 4..89
Rules of the Supreme Court 1965 (SI No 1776)
    Order 53.. 106

Secure Tenants of Local Authorities (Compensation for
   Improvements) Regulations 1994...37

Declarations and Determinations

Housing (Rent to Mortgage) (Multipliers and Relevant Amount)
   Declaration 1996..66

Housing (Right to Buy) (Cost Floor) Determinations 1992............ 61

Housing (Right to Buy) (Cost Floor) Determinations 1993............ 61

Introduction

The "right to buy" for social housing tenants was introduced by the Housing Act 1980. At various times since then the mechanisms have been altered to encourage further council tenants and some housing association tenants to becoming home owners. More than 1.42 million tenants bought their homes from English local authorities and new towns between April 1979 and December 1994 (HL Debs. col 249, 17 May 1995). About a tenth of those are now long lease-holders; the remainder have purchased the freehold. The Housing Act 1996 reinforced the commitment to the right to buy, with new rights to acquire for tenants of regis-tered social landlords.

There has been much opposition to the right to buy. There was initial opposition from local authorities who wished to resist the depletion of their stock. This problem was foreseen in the legislation which gave the Secretary of State draconian powers to intervene to ensure sales took place.

After the initial wave of enthusiasm for home owner-ship amongst tenants, some have found themselves bur-dened with responsibilities they cannot cope with, and properties they cannot sell. Landlords have found difficulties in managing stock which has been bought on long leases.

The current legislation is found in the Housing Act 1985, although there have been further amendments to this by the Housing and Planning Act 1986 and the Leasehold Reform, Housing and Urban Development Act 1993 with effect from 11 October 1993. The basic scheme of the 1985 Act now gives secure tenants (subject to certain exceptions) the right to buy their home. Essentially tenants of houses have the right to acquire the freehold, and tenants of flats the leasehold, at a price discounted in accordance with the length of time that the tenant has been a public sector tenant.

Despite the Act's fairly basic structure, the provisions are themselves very complex. The intention of this book is to enable those who work in social housing, who may be called upon to answer questions from tenants about the right to buy, to understand the operation of the Act. While those administering the right to buy may be familiar with the operation of parts of the Act, it is hoped that the book will also enable them to understand the overall operation and some of the legal issues to which their work may give rise.

The book sets out the Act as it currently operates (at the time of writing) for those applying under the right to buy. To have dealt with every possible situation under earlier legislation would have made it impossibly long and complex. Given the many amendments which have been made to the scheme over the years, where disputes arise over earlier applications, it should be remembered that the applicable law may be different as applications must be assessed in accordance with the law in force at the time they were made.

The first chapter deals with entitlement to the right to buy, which is given to secure tenants, to joint tenants and to their family members. Chapter 2 explains how the qualifying period is calculated, and lists the exceptions to the right to buy.

Chapter 3 describes the type of interest which may be granted to the tenant (i.e. whether the tenant is entitled to buy the leasehold or the freehold). The legal definitions of "house" and "flat" are considered.

The complex procedure for exercising the right to buy is summarised in Chapter 4, with certain problems or potential problems highlighted. The service of notices both generally and in the context of exercising the right is also dealt with here. There is a section on dealing with delays in the procedure and action which may be taken by landlord or tenant to speed things up.

Chapter 5 discusses how the purchase price, which is the most important element for the potential purchaser, is calculated through valuing the property and deducting the discount to which the tenant is entitled. The chapter also discusses the right to acquire on rent to mortgage terms, introduced in 1993 to replace the rights to a mortgage and to a shared ownership lease. The new scheme has been taken up with less enthusiasm than the government anticipated. It has attracted only a handful of tenants (see the DoE report *Evaluation of the pilot rents to mortgage scheme*, HMSO). Few people qualify because of the requirement that the tenant does not receive housing benefit.

Chapter 6 considers the preparation of the grant or conveyance; the liability to repay the discount; and the "reasonableness" requirement of public sector landlords in introducing certain covenants to achieve uniformity in the leaseholders' terms and conditions. Much publicity has been given to the problems faced by purchasers particularly in respect of service charges. Inadequate information for tenants at the time of purchase, the poor quality of construction of much social housing and "mortgage blight" have been blamed in some cases. The difficulties faced by leaseholders and the legal position on the recovery of service charges are beyond the scope of this book (but see *Leaseholder Management*, D Kilcoyne (Arden's Housing Library) 1997).

Chapter 7 focuses on the circumstances in which tenants may lose the right to buy; enforcement; and situations in which a secure tenant's status is lost. (There is detailed treatment of this in A Dymond, *Security of Tenure* (Arden's Housing Library) 1995.)

The effect of a change of landlord is described in Chapter 8. Methods of dispute resolution are also considered, including applications for judicial review and the Secretary of State's powers to intervene. The preserved right to buy is also given detailed treatment in that chapter.

Where the landlord is not the property owner, the tenant may be able to buy the freehold directly from the freeholder. The landlord has certain responsibilities in acting as a "go-between". This is known as the extension of the right to buy, and is explained in Chapter 9.

The position of housing associations and other registered social landlords is discussed in Chapter 10. While the secure tenants of some housing associations have the right to buy, others do not. Furthermore there was no equivalent right where the tenancy was granted after 15 January 1989 and accordingly assured. Some assistance has been available to tenants to buy elsewhere, however, through the "tenants' incentive scheme". The Housing Act 1996 more sweepingly introduced the new right to acquire, which is applicable to all registered social landlords. This seems unlikely, however, to give rise to a flood of applications. In the 15 or so years since the right to buy was made available for the 500 or so charitable associations, just under a quarter (35,000) of the 150,000 tenants entitled to buy have done so (Peter Mason, *Inside Housing* 12 May 1995). Many tenants will be on housing benefit or have already participated in a tenants' incentive scheme; which has enabled those who can afford to buy to do so in the private market. There has been much objection to the extension. Some housing associations have a mixed portfolio of properties and fear that the cream of their stock will be acquired by tenants. The right to acquire could reduce an association's borrowing power and income from rents.

1.

Who Has the Right to Buy?

Secure tenants / Joint tenants /
Family members

The main prerequisite which entitles someone to the right to buy is a secure tenancy. This chapter considers the requirements of a secure tenancy and of a joint secure tenancy, and of a secure tenant's family members' right to buy.

Secure tenants

The right to buy is primarily given to secure tenants (HA 1985, s 118(1)). It is very important therefore to consider whether a right to buy applicant fulfils this very basic requirement. A brief outline is set out here, but for a detailed consideration readers are referred to A Dymond, *Security of Tenure*, (Arden's Housing Library) 1995.

Requirements of a secure tenancy.

The five conditions for a secure tenancy are as follows:

1. the accommodation must be a dwelling-house (HA 1985, s 112);

2. the accommodation must be let as a separate dwelling;

3. the tenant condition must be satisfied (HA 1985, s 81);

4. the landlord condition for a secure tenancy must be satisfied (HA 1985, s 80);

5. the tenancy must not be excluded from security under Schedule 1 to HA 1985.

The tenant condition

The tenant condition under **3.** above is that the tenant is an individual (not a company or a trustee, for example) and occupies the dwelling-house as his or her only or principal home. (For a consideration of whether the dwelling-house is the tenant's only or principal home see for example *Crawley Borough Council v Sawyer* (1987) 20 HLR 98.) It is not necessary for there to be actual physical occupation of the home. A tenant may continue to occupy a dwelling-house after he or she has left if his or her spouse remains in occupation (Matrimonial Homes Act 1983, s 1(6); Family Law Act 1996 s 30(4)).

A licensee does not have the right to buy. Where the landlord condition is satisfied (see below) but the occupier holds a licence rather than a tenancy, the occupier may be treated as a tenant for the purposes of Part IV of HA 1985 (security of tenure) but not for the purposes of Part V (right to buy). This comes from the wording of section 79(3) of the Act (defining those licences which are secure). For the difference between a tenancy and a licence see the discussion in A Dymond, *Security of Tenure* (Arden's Housing Library) Chapter 2.

The landlord condition

The landlord condition under **4.** above is that the landlord is one of the following:

- a local authority
- a new town corporation

- a housing action trust (since 15 November 1988)
- an urban development corporation
- the Development Board for Rural Wales
- certain co-operative housing associations

(HA 1985, s 27B).

Section 80 of the 1985 Act was amended by the Housing Act 1988. If the tenancy was granted before 15 January 1989, the following landlords also satisfy the landlord condition:

- the Housing Corporation
- charitable housing trusts
- certain registered housing associations.

Those tenants did not lose secure status when their landlords ceased to satisfy the landlord condition and they remain secure tenants. See Chapter 10 on housing associations and the right to buy.

Tenancies that are not secure

In outline, a tenancy which would otherwise be secure is not, in one of a dozen circumstances as follows:

1. it is a long tenancy (i.e. generally more than 21 years);

2. the dwelling-house is occupied in connection with certain employments;

3. the dwelling-house is on land which has been acquired for development and it is used in the meantime as temporary housing accommodation;

4. the tenancy was granted as temporary accommodation in pursuance of certain duties to the homeless under either:

(a) Part III of the Housing Act 1985 and less than 12 months has expired (unless there has been notification of a secure tenancy), or

(b) Part VII of the Housing Act 1996 (unless the tenant has been notified that the tenancy is to be secure);

5. the tenancy was granted as temporary accommodation to allow the tenant to take up employment in the area and find permanent accommodation and

(a) in the case of a local housing authority the tenant has not been notified that the tenancy is to be secure, or

(b) in the case of other secure landlords less than 12 months has expired (provided that the tenant was not, immediately before the grant, resident in the district and that he was notified that the exception applies and unless there has been notification of a secure tenancy);

6. the dwelling-house was leased to the landlord under certain short-term arrangements (i.e. it was leased or licensed with vacant possession for use as temporary accommodation);

7. the dwelling-house has been made available to the tenant, or a predecessor, while works are carried out on his home of which he was not a secure tenant;

8. the dwelling-house is part of certain agricultural holdings and occupied by the person in control of the farming;

9. the dwelling-house consists of or includes licensed premises;

10. the tenancy was granted to allow the tenant to attend certain educational courses and

(a) in the case of local housing authority the tenant has not been notified that the tenancy is to be secure, or

(b) in the case of other secure landlords less than a certain period has expired (provided the tenant was notified that the exception applies and unless there has been notification of a secure tenancy);

11. the tenancy is one to which Part II of the Landlord and Tenant Act 1954 applies (tenancies of premises occupied for business purposes);

12. occupation is by virtue of a licence granted by an almshouse charity in certain circumstances.

Even if the section 80 landlord condition is satisfied (and the tenancy is not exempt by virtue of Schedule 1), there may be exemption from the right to buy scheme under Schedule 5 to the Housing Act 1985. See Chapter 2.

Tenancy connected with employment

The tenancy is not secure if the tenant is an employee of the landlord or of certain other public bodies (i.e. a local authority, a new town corporation, a housing action trust, an urban development corporation, the Development Board for Rural Wales, or the governors of an aided school), and his contract of employment requires him to occupy the dwelling-house for the better performance of his duties. A number of cases have considered this issue where the tenant has sought to exercise the right to buy.

Case report

Mr Hughes, headmaster of a boarding school, was provided with a house close to the school by the Inner London Education Authority, whose successors were the London Borough of Greenwich. Under his contract of employment there was no express requirement that Mr Hughes lived in the house for the better performance of his duties, although it was convenient for him and the authority that he did so. Following his retirement Mr Hughes sought to exercise the right to buy the house.

The authority contended that Mr Hughes was not a secure tenant because of the exception relating to employment. The House of Lords refused to imply a term into his contract that the house was essential for the performance of his duties, and accordingly the exception did not apply. As a secure tenant Mr Hughes had the right to buy. *Hughes v Greenwich London Borough Council* [1993] 3 WLR 821, (1994) 26 HLR 99.

Once the tenant has ceased his employment he may acquire a secure status if he is allowed to remain in the accommodation for a significant period (see *South Glamorgan County Council v Griffiths* (1992) 24 HLR 334; *Campbell v City of*

Edinburgh District Council 1987 SLT 51; *Greenfield v Berkshire County Council* (1996) 28 HLR 691). It is very important for secure landlords to consider the position of employees in tied accommodation when either their employment is terminated or their employment contract terms are changed, since this may have significant implications on their right to buy accommodation which may be needed for other employees.

A tenant is not a secure tenant if he or she lives in accommodation provided by the police or fire authority.

Short-term lease arrangements

Under condition **6.** above (dwelling-house leased or licensed with vacant possession to a landlord for use as temporary accommodation), vacant possession is obtained from the landlord on expiry of the lease or as required by the lessor. The lessor must not be a body which is capable of granting secure tenancies in its own right. The landlord must have no other interest in the dwelling-house apart from a mortgage.

Loss of security

A tenant may lose security at any time. For example security is lost when a tenant sublets the whole of his or her tenancy (HA 1985, s 93(2)). The implications of loss of security on the right to buy are considered in Chapter 7.

As well as once and for all loss of security, a tenant may swing in and out of security. For example a sole tenant loses security if he or she ceases to occupy the dwelling-house as his or her only or principal home (and his or her spouse does not occupy it either), but this may be regained by subsequent reoccupation (*Hussey v London Borough of Camden* (1994) 27 HLR 5, CA). Similarly an exception in Schedule 1 may cease to apply because of a change of circumstances.

Case report

In 1978 Mr Elvidge was employed by Coventry City Council as a water bailiff in a country park. In 1979 he was offered a tenancy of a property known as "Highfields", which was situated in the park. Mr Elvidge signed a document by which he agreed that his right to occupy would cease should his employment cease, but his employment contract did not expressly require him to live in the cottage. In 1983 Mr Elvidge was promoted to assistant ranger; he took on more duties and was paid a higher salary. In particular he was then required to live in the park for the better performance of his duties.

In 1990 Mr Elvidge sought to exercise his right to buy. The council denied this right on the basis that he was not a secure tenant because of the exception in Schedule 1, paragraph 2 to the Housing Act 1985 (i.e. because of the "better performance of his duties" requirement). Mr Elvidge sought a declaration that he was entitled to exercise the right. At trial the judge found that when the tenancy had first been granted it had been secure, but that the change in his terms of employment in 1983 brought it within the exception in paragraph 2 and it was therefore not a secure tenancy at the relevant date. He dismissed the application and Mr Elvidge appealed.

The Court of Appeal agreed with the judgment and held that the exception could apply from time to time, so that at the time of his application to exercise the right to buy Mr Elvidge was not a secure tenant. *Elvidge v Coventry City Council* (1993) 26 HLR 281, CA.

This case illustrates the need to consider whether a particular applicant is a secure tenant at the time of the application for the right to buy. It should not be assumed, simply because that at some time the tenancy was secure, that it necessarily is now.

Joint tenants

Where a secure tenancy is a joint tenancy, the right to buy belongs to all the tenants, even if they are not living on the premises (HA 1985, s 118(2)). Each joint tenant must be an individual but only one need occupy the dwelling-house as his or her only or principal home. Where a joint tenant leaves the home the tenancy is not automatically determined (even if he or she is forced to leave by an ouster injunction). Unless he or she surrenders or releases his or her interest, the absent tenant remains secure and retains the right to buy so long as one tenant is in occupation.

Sometimes one or more of the tenants may not wish to be involved. The tenants may decide amongst themselves that the right to buy will belong to one or more of them as agreed. At least one of those persons nominated must occupy the dwelling-house as his or her only or principal home. There are no provisions about the form of the agreement between the tenants and the general law of contract applies. It seems the landlord may accept the word of just one tenant but can require evidence of the agreement in writing.

Loss of right by a joint tenant

If a joint tenant of a periodic (e.g. weekly) tenancy serves a valid notice to quit, the tenancy is determined even if the other tenant objects (see further, A Dymond, *Security of Tenure* (Arden's Housing Library) 1995, chapter 12).

Where there is a breakdown in the relationship between tenants, the landlord usually grants a new sole tenancy to the remaining tenant. A joint tenant may also lose his or her tenancy if there is a property transfer order made under the Matrimonial Causes Act 1973, the Matrimonial Homes Act 1983 (or the Family Law Act 1996 when it comes into force) or the Children Act 1989. A tenant might lose security if an ouster injunction (or occupation order) is made against him or her for a long period. It is therefore important that in any settlement or order made under these Acts, the right to buy implications are considered.

Family members

The right to buy may be shared with up to three members of the secure tenant's family (HA 1985, s 123). It is not clear whether joint tenants can each share the right to buy with three family members (thus, in the case of two joint tenants, making eight potential purchasers). A maximum of four persons can own land under the Law of Property Act 1925, section 34 and the Trustee Act 1925, section 34. Therefore if more than four persons wish to share the right to buy, the remainder can only be granted an equitable interest. The first four persons named in the grant become joint tenants of the legal estate, holding an implied trust of land for all the grantees as tenants in common of the equitable interest. For this reason some legal commentators suggest that the right to join family members is limited to a maximum of three or less where there are joint tenants.

If the tenant wishes to share his or her right to buy he or she must say so in the section 122 notice. Once the tenant has served notice that he or she wishes to share the right to buy with a member of his or her family with whom he or she has a right to share, that person must be treated as a joint secure tenant (HA 1985, s 123(3)). The effect of this is that even if the secure tenant dies, the nominated family member(s) can still proceed with the right to buy.

Case report

Mrs Tonge succeeded to a secure tenancy on her husband's death in 1976. In 1988 she sought to exercise the right to buy, and nominated her daughter as a family member sharing the right to buy. All matters as to the exercise of the right to buy were agreed with the council by June

1989, but Mrs Tonge and her daughter decided to defer completion (as they were then entitled to do under the legislation), and paid the appropriate deposit. In November 1990 Mrs Tonge died. Her daughter wished, however, to complete the conveyance in April 1991. The council refused stating that as she had no right to succeed to the secure tenancy, her right to buy had also lapsed. The Court of Appeal held that as she was deemed to be a joint secure tenant, her rights continued after her mother's death, and she was entitled to enforce the right. *London Borough of Harrow v Tonge* (1992) 25 HLR 99.

Who is a family member?

A person is a member of another person's family under HA 1985, section 186 if:

    1. he or she is the spouse of that person, or he or she and that person live together as husband and wife, or
    2. he or she is that person's parent, grandparent, child, grandchild, brother, sister, uncle, aunt, nephew or niece.

The definition under **1.** above has been construed strictly. It has been held that the expression "living together as husband and wife" does not include a homosexual relationship (*Harrogate Borough Council v Simpson* (1984) 17 HLR 205) so a local authority may not extend the right to buy to allow it to be shared with lesbian and gay partners. There is no prohibition against sharing the right to buy with children. Persons under 18 cannot hold a legal estate in land (Law of Property Act 1925, s 19) but by sections19(2) and 35 of the Law of Property Act 1925 the conveyance or grant will be to all those persons of 18 or over, to be held on a statutory trust for those persons and all those under 18.

    On the other hand the definition in **2.** above is a wide one. Section 186 states:

"For the purposes of [this definition] (a) a relationship by marriage shall be treated as a relationship by blood, (b) a relationship of the half-blood shall be treated as a relationship of the whole blood, (c) the stepchild of a person shall be treated as his child, and (d) an illegitimate child shall be treated as the legitimate child of his mother and reputed father."

Occupying requirements

All the family members who are added to the application must occupy the dwelling-house as their only or principal home. There is no requirement that a family member should be an occupant authorised by the landlord.

There is a further residential qualification for all family members who are not the tenant's spouse. A family member must have been residing with the secure tenant throughout the 12-month period ending with the giving of the section 122 notice. There is a similar residential qualification for persons succeeding to a secure tenancy under HA 1985, section 87 which is dealt with in detail in C Hunter, *Tenants' Rights* (Arden's Housing Library) 1995, Chapter 2.

2.

Qualifications and Exceptions

The qualifying period./
Exceptions to right to buy

Even if the tenant is secure, he or she will not qualify for the right to buy if:

   (a) the qualification period has not been fulfilled, or
   (b) if the tenancy falls within one of a number of exceptions.

The qualifying period

The right to buy does not arise unless the two-year qualification period has elapsed (HA 1985, s 119). The period is calculated in accordance with the provisions of Schedule 4 to HA 1985. The two years need not be spent in the same premises and need not be continuous, although the tenant must be a secure tenant at the time he or she makes the claim and, usually, at the time of grant (see Chapter 7). Although a licensee does not have the right to buy (see Chapter 1), occupation under a licence counts for the qualification period as if it was under a tenancy (unless the licence was granted as a temporary expedient to someone who entered as a trespasser (HA 1985, Sched 4, para 6). Where there is a secure joint tenancy, only one tenant need qualify.

Relevant periods

The following periods must be taken into account in calculating the two-year qualification period:

Secure tenant

Any relevant period during which the secure tenant was a "public sector tenant".

Secure tenant and spouse

Any period during which a tenant's spouse was a public sector tenant, if at the time of making his or her claim the tenant is living with a spouse. The tenant need not have been living with his or her spouse during the qualifying time as long as they are living together at the time of the claim.

> **Example**
>
> Mr Patel lived in private rented accommodation. In January 1992 he got married and moved in with his wife, who had been a sole secure tenant of a one-bedroom council flat in Camden since January 1985. They had two children and in January 1996 they were transferred by the council to a three bedroom flat, in the sole name of Mr Patel. In February 1996 he claimed the right to buy. The qualifying period (January 1985 to January 1996) is eleven years, even though Mr Patel himself has only been a public sector tenant for less than one year.

Deceased tenant – the widow(er)'s right to buy

Any period during which a deceased spouse was a public sector tenant, if at the time of death they were living together. Again they need not have been living together during the period.

> **Example**
>
> Mrs White claims the right to buy her flat where she has lived on her own for a year since her husband died. She was made homeless from the private flat she occupied with her husband before he died. Ten years ago, her husband was a council tenant for two years before he moved into private sector housing. Although Mrs White never lived with her deceased husband in his council flat, the qualifying period is three years.

Where spouse is a public sector tenant

Any period during which the secure tenant lived with his or her spouse who was a public sector tenant. The secure tenant must have occupied his or her spouse's home as his or her only or principal home for the whole period to be counted. It does not matter whether the parties are living together at the time of claim.

> **Example**
>
> Mrs Tan is separated from her husband. Before she was granted the tenancy of her council flat last month, she lived with her husband in a council house of which he was the sole tenant. Although he had been living in the house for ten years, and they had been living together for four of those years, she lived with him for only a year after they were married, after which they separated. Because they are not living together at the time of applying for the right to buy, his occupation on his own does not count. The qualifying period is a year, because that is the only period during which they lived together after they were married. She was not a tenant during that year, but she was the spouse of a tenant and she occupied the house as her only or principal home.

In some cases where the secure tenant's spouse had a previous marriage the following further periods must be taken into account:

Where previous spouse was a public sector tenant

Any period during which the secure tenant's current spouse (i.e. the person with whom he or she lives at the time of making the claim) lived with a previous spouse who was a public sector tenant. The current spouse must have occupied his or her previous spouse's home as his or her only or principal home for the whole period to be counted.

> **Example**
>
> Mrs McKibben has been the sole tenant of the council house, which she occupies with her husband, since they married last year. Ten years ago, Mr McKibben lived for a year with his first wife in council accommodation in her sole name. The qualifying period is two years.

Deceased spouse's previous marriage

Any period during which the secure tenant's deceased spouse (if they were living together at the time of death) lived with a spouse who was a public sector tenant. The current spouse must have occupied his or her previous spouse's home as his or her only or principal home for the whole period to be counted.

> **Example**
>
> Mr Gore applies for the right to buy after living only one year in his flat. He married his wife 15 years ago; it was her second marriage, and she died earlier this year. They were provided with council accommodation last year after living for 15 years in the private sector. Mr Gore has never lived in council accommodation before last year, as a tenant or otherwise, but 20 years ago his wife lived with her first husband in his council flat for five years. The qualifying period is six years.

There are further periods which may need to be taken into account in certain circumstances:

Acquiring tenancy of parent's home

Where a public sector tenant takes over the tenancy of the home of a parent (who was also a public sector tenant) or is granted a new tenancy of the same dwelling-house, any period during which he or she occupied the dwelling-house as his or her only or principal home either:

    1. up to the time when he or she was granted the tenancy (and since reaching the age of 16), or
    2. up to the time when he or she left so long as it was no more than two years before being granted the tenancy (or any public sector tenancy qualification period as above).

It was held in a Scottish case on similar provisions that it is only the immediate succession which counts. The tenant cannot claim time in respect of the tenancy before the last one to which he or she succeeded (*Hamilton v City of Glasgow District Council* 1996 SLT (Lands Tr) 14, reported in *Current Law*, May 1996).

> ### Example
>
> Ms Ballinira succeeded to her mother's tenancy when she was 24 years old. She has lived in the house all her life, save when she was living away from home at university at ages 19-21, and for a year after that when she moved out and lived with her boyfriend after an argument with her mother. The qualifying period is the sum of the two years when she was living there between the ages of 16 and 18, probably the three years she was at university, if she was "in digs" and still regarded her mother's home as her only or principal home, and the last two years since she returned after the argument, giving a total of seven years. The year she lived with her boyfriend will probably not count.

Armed forces accommodation

A period where a tenant occupies forces accommodation must be taken into account if provided to the tenant, his spouse or deceased spouse as a member of the regular armed forces.

"Reserved" periods

There are periods during which the right to buy is preserved, these must be taken into account; see Chapter 9 below.

Public sector tenant

"Public sector tenant" is defined in paragraph 6 of Schedule 4 to HA 1985. The concept of public sector tenant is defined in similar terms to a secure tenancy, with a landlord and a tenant condition. However, the landlord condition is defined much more broadly.

References to public sector tenant include a joint tenant so long as he or she occupied the dwelling-house as his or her only or principal home. The tenancy must not be a "long tenancy" (essentially a tenancy for a term exceeding 21 years) (HA 1985, ss 187, 115). There are two criteria to be satisfied: the landlord condition and the tenant condition. The tenant condition is the same as that used to determine a secure tenant (HA 1985, Sched 4, paras 7-9).

The landlord condition

The landlord condition for the qualifying period is similar to that used to determine a secure tenant, and includes:

- a local authority;
- a new town corporation;
- a housing trust (since 15 November 1988);
- the Development Board for Rural Wales;
- an urban development corporation.

But unlike the landlord condition for a secure tenancy it also includes the following:

- the Housing Corporation, Scottish Homes or Housing for Wales;
- a registered social landlord which is not a co-operative housing association;
- corresponding authorities in Scotland and Northern Ireland;
- certain co-operative housing associations, i.e. property let under a housing co-operative agreement made by a local housing authority, new town corporation or the Development Board for Rural Wales;
- authorities and bodies prescribed by the Secretary of State.

The list of Secretary of State prescribed bodies is long, and currently contained in the Housing (Right to Buy) (Prescribed Persons) Order 1992 (SI No 1703) which includes for example a government department, a parish council, the Post Office, etc. The Secretary of State may add further landlords to the list.

Exceptions to right to buy

Even where the applicant is a secure tenant and fulfils the qualification period, the right to buy does not arise if the tenancy falls within one of the exceptions set out in Schedule 5 to the 1985 Act. These are the only permitted exceptions to the right to buy (HA 1985, s 120). A landlord cannot prevent the right to buy arising by agreement, nor prohibit it by a term in the tenancy, since any such prohibition or restriction is treated as void (HA 1985, s 179(1)).

Excepted landlords

The right to buy does not arise if the landlord is:

- a housing trust which is a charity (this includes trustees holding on charitable trusts for housing purposes;

■ a housing association which is a charity;
■ a co-operative housing association;
■ a housing association which has never received certain grants (the list in Schedule 5 to the 1985 Act should be consulted in case of doubt);
■ a Crown tenant (unless the landlord is entitled to grant a lease in pursuance of the right to buy, or the appropriate consent is obtained).

Housing associations are discussed further in Chapter 10.

Insufficient interest in property

An exception arises if the landlord has insufficient interest in the property (HA 1985, Sched 5, para 4). If the property is a house, the landlord must own either the freehold or a leasehold interest exceeding 21 years. If the property is a flat, it must own either the freehold or a leasehold interest of 50 years or more. In ascertaining the length of the interest, the time runs from the date of the tenant's notice claiming the right to buy.

It appears from *R v Council of the City of Plymouth and Cornwall County Council, ex p John Charles Freeman* (1986) 18 HLR 243 that a council may avoid the right to buy by creating a short lease of the property to be held by another landlord so that the landlord condition is no longer satisfied. However since the *Plymouth* case was decided, tenants have been given the right to buy the freehold under the Housing (Extension of Right to Buy) Order 1987, so long as all the intermediate interests are held by prescribed landlords (see para 3(2) of the 1987 Order).

Excepted property

Employment-related tenancy

The right to buy does not arise if the dwelling-house forms part, or is within the curtilage, of another building which is held by the landlord mainly for purposes other than housing (i.e. not under Part II of HA 1985), and the dwelling is let to the tenant or a predecessor *in consequence* of his or her employment by the landlord or certain other public bodies (HA 1985, Sched 4, para 5). If the tenant is *required* to occupy the accommodation for the better performance of his or her duties, he or she is a service occupier and does not have the right to buy in any event, as the licence under which he or she occupies is not secure.

A building is within the "curtilage" of another if it forms "part and parcel" of the other building. It must be at least adjacent to the other building (*Barwick and Barwick v Kent County Council* (1992) 24 HLR 341). In *Dyer v Dorset County Council* [1989] QB 346 a staff house in college grounds was held not to be within the curtilage of the college building.

Case report

Mr Barwick was a fireman, and in consequence of his employment he was offered the tenancy of a house by Kent County Council. It was not, however, a condition of his employment that he lived in the house for the better performance of his duties. The house was near to the fire station, which was a large building with a large yard to the rear. At the back of the yard was a row of garages. At the end of the garages there was a high brick wall, through which a number of gates led to the gardens of ten houses, one of which was that occupied by Mr Barwick. All the houses were built at the same time as the fire station for the purpose of housing firemen, and formed a small "housing estate".

In 1987 Mr Barwick and his wife applied to exercise the right to buy. The county council denied the right on the basis that the house fell within the exception in paragraph 5 of Schedule 4. The question which arose was whether the house fell within the curtilage of the fire station. The Court of Appeal held that it did not, since it fell outside the clearly defined boundary wall, which formed the curtilage. The court stated that what is included in the curtilage is narrower than something which it is convenient to have for the use of the relevant building. It must be immediately ad-jacent to that building. *Barwick and Barwick v Kent County Council* (1992) 24 HLR 341.

If not employed by the landlord, the other bodies which the tenant may be employed by are a local authority, a new town corporation, a housing action trust, the Development Board for Rural Wales, an urban development corporation or the governors of an aided school. Dwelling-houses within cemeteries are also excluded from the right to buy.

Dwelling-houses for disabled tenants

Physically disabled   For the physically disabled, a dwelling-house is exempt if all of the following criteria are satisfied:

   1. it has features which are substantially different from those of ordinary dwelling-houses;
   2. those features are designed to make the dwelling-house suitable for occupation by physically disabled persons;
   3. the dwelling-house is one of a group usually let for occupation by physically disabled persons;
   4. social services or special facilities are provided for the occupants in close proximity to the group (HA 1985, Sched 4, para 6).

The question of whether the features are substantially different under **1.** above is one of common sense.

Case report

Mr and Mrs Freeman were tenants of Wansbeck District Council. Their daughter suffered from spina bifida, and as a consequence a small downstairs toilet was installed by

> the council in the house, since she had difficulty climbing
> the stairs. The Freemans sought to exercise their right to
> buy, which the council denied on the basis that the house
> fell within the exception for disabled persons (which at
> that time also applied to single dwellings as well as
> groups). It was held that the downstairs toilet was not suf-
> ficient to bring the house within the exemption, as it was
> not a substantially different feature. The Court of Appeal
> suggested that the exemption would apply if there were
> structural adaptations such as the provision of ramps,
> widened doors or alteration of cooking and working
> surfaces. *Freeman v Wansbeck District Council* [1984]
> 2 All ER 746.

Mentally disabled   For persons who suffer or have suffered
from a mental disorder (as defined in the Mental Health Act
1983), a dwelling-house is exempt with or without special
features. The only criteria that must be satisfied are **3.** (for
mentally rather than physically disabled), and **4.** above.

Dwelling-houses for elderly tenants

A dwelling-house is exempt if all the following criteria are
satisfied:

1. it is one of a group particularly suitable for occupation by elderly persons; to determine particular suitability
regard must be had to "its location, size, design, heating system and other features";

2. the dwelling-houses in a group are usually let
to persons aged 60 or more; the dwelling-houses need
not be intended for letting exclusively to the elderly if
the other occupants are intended to be persons with a
physical disability;

3. the group is warden controlled; if the warden is
not resident, there must be a system for calling him or her
and the use of a nearby common room (HA 1985, Sched 4,
para 10).

The exception also applies to single dwellings but only if the dwelling-house is particularly suitable (see **1.** above) and it was let before 1 January 1990 for occupation by a person aged 60 or more, either to the present tenant or his or her predecessor (HA 1985, Sched 4, para 11). The elderly person need not be the tenant – he or she could be, for example, the tenant's parent – but the elderly person must be specified as an intended occupant at the time of the letting. Criterion **1.** above must be satisfied for an individual house rather than a group. Any features provided by the tenant or a predecessor are to be disregarded.

It is for the local authority to decide whether a dwelling-house falls within the exception. If the tenant is not happy with the decision, he or she may apply, within 56 days of service of the section 124 notice, to the Secretary of State for the matter to be determined. Before amendment by the Leasehold Reform, Housing and Urban Development Act 1993, in respect of claims made between 1 March 1990 and 11 October 1993, a landlord would first have to obtain a determination from the Secretary of State that an application fell within one of the exceptions. If the determination was not received from the Secretary of State the exception could not apply. Guidance for deciding whether homes are particularly suitable for accommodating persons of pensionable age are set out in DoE Circular 3/90. The criteria were to be used by the Secretary of State, but the same criteria should now be followed by local authorities when making the decision themselves.

There are criteria in the DoE Circular concerning the property itself. If the criteria are not followed carefully and proper enquiries are not made in respect of each of them, the decision may be challenged. A decision which departed from the policy was successfully challenged (see the case report below). This was a case decided before amendment by the 1993 Act but the principles apply to decision-making by the landlord.

Case report

Mrs Bint, a pensioner, applied to buy her home in a small village where there were no shops selling basic foodstuff. One of the criteria in the DoE Circular is that to fall within the exception the dwelling-house should be "located reasonably conveniently for shops and public transport, *having regard to the nature of the area*". The emphasised words were included in response to concerns from the Association of District Councils that, if applied to rural areas, many dwellings would fall outside the criteria. In this case, the Secretary of State did not consider the nature of the area but took a more rigid approach, stating that in general "a round trip of two miles to the nearest shop, carrying shopping on the return journey, is too far for a person of pensionable age". The Secretary of State's decision that the house did not fall within the exception was quashed. *R v Secretary of State for the Environment, ex p West Oxfordshire District Council* (1993) 26 HLR 417.

3.
What is Bought?

The dwelling-house / House or flat /
Interest to be conveyed or granted

The tenant's basic entitlement is to the freehold or the leasehold of his or her dwelling-house (HA 1985, s 118). Which of
these may be acquired depends on two factors: the interest
owned by the landlord; and whether the dwelling is a house
or a flat. On the first point it should be remembered that the
landlord must have a minimum interest of a lease beyond a
certain number of years before the tenant may acquire at all.

Before considering the legal interest in the property
which the tenant may acquire, two other issues must be considered: how the property is to be defined (e.g. what land
may be included); and how flats and houses are defined.

The dwelling-house

The basic right is to acquire the dwelling-house. The
dwelling-house is the whole property let to the tenant
(HA 1985, s 183). This includes the building and all the land
that is let with it (but not agricultural land exceeding two
acres). Other land must also be treated as included in a
dwelling house if:

- it has been used for the purpose of the dwelling-
  house; and

■ if the tenant serves written notice (the section 184 notice) before exercising the right to buy (or the right to acquire on rent to mortgage terms) that he or she wants the land to be included; and

■ if it is reasonable in all the circumstances for the land to be included (HA 1985, s 184).

The landlord cannot refuse to include the land if all the above criteria are satisfied. If there is a dispute the matter may be resolved in the county court under section 181.

The tenant may serve the section 184 notice at any time, even after service of the landlord's section 125 notice. The tenant must not be penalised for the late service of the section 184 notice, but rather the parties must take all such steps as are necessary to achieve the position they would have been in had the notice been served prior to the section 125 notice (HA 1985, s 184(4)). Thus the section 125 notice (and any other notices which have been served) will probably need to be amended or withdrawn and reserved, as clearly the valuation of the property will be affected by the inclusion of extra land. It may be necessary to extend time limits for service so that the tenant and landlord are put in the same position as if the notice had been served on time. If a tenant changes his or her mind, he or she may withdraw the section 184 notice at any time. If the notice is withdrawn after service of the section 125 notice, the necessary steps must be taken to put the parties in the same position as they would have been in had the notice been withdrawn at the beginning of the procedure.

House or flat

Every dwelling-house must be either a "house" or a "flat", as defined in section 183 of HA 1985. The section gives a lengthy definition of "house" and then defines every dwelling-house which is not a house as a "flat".

The reasonableness test

The basic definition of house in section 183 is that a house is "a structure reasonably so called". Thus in many respects it is a matter of common sense whether something is a house or not. There have been no reported cases on this provision, although there have been disputes under the Leasehold Reform Act 1967, which includes a similar definition, where it has been said that the question is a mixed one of fact and law. Any dispute can be resolved by reference to the county court (HA 1985, s 181).

Following from the broad definition, section 183 describes three situations and states whether in each case the dwelling-house can be described as a house. The first situation gives rise to a clear definition, but the second and third situations are more in the nature of guidelines.

Horizontal division

The first situation is "where a building is divided horizontally, the flats or other units into which it is divided are not houses". This is perhaps the most common and obvious situation, in that when a building is split up into separate dwellings, on different levels, each dwelling will be called a flat. "Divided" means divided into separate dwelling-houses. In *Sharpe v Duke Street Securities* (1987) 19 HLR 506, a case decided under the Leasehold Reform Act 1967 which allows private sector tenants to buy the freehold or an extended lease of their homes, a building which was divided into two flats but which was connected up and lived in as a single residence was held to be a house.

Vertical division

The second situation is "where a building is divided vertically, the units into which it is divided may be houses". This part suggests that a vertical division may result in two "houses" but the overriding test is still one of reasonableness. Some conversions may lead to vertical splits, but it is necessary to consider carefully in such situations whether the division has created flats or houses. Probably where the building is split part vertically and part horizontally, or where a building is divided horizontally but each flat has its own front door, each dwelling will be a flat. What is clear from this definition (if there were any doubt) is that in a standard row of terraced houses, each will be a "house".

Material part over remainder of structure

The third situation is "where a building is not structurally detached, it is not a house if a material part of it lies above or below the remainder of the structure". This problematical part suggests that, for example, flats above or below offices or shops are usually treated as flats. The whole building cannot be considered a house. Nor can there be a house where only part of the dwelling extends over the other building, even if the dwelling has the appearance of being a house.

The residents of a building which is divided into flats cannot join together and claim to buy the freehold of the whole building on the ground that it is a "house". Section 183 makes it clear that "house" and "flat" are sub-species of "dwelling-house" – so, for example, a building divided into flats is a building containing several dwelling-houses. It is not a house in its own right.

It seems that the overriding, central test is whether the structure is "reasonably so called". The three definitions in section 183(2)(a)-(c) are not sufficient in their own right but are examples or consequences or applications of the central definition. Thus even if a building is not divided and is structurally detached the court might say that it is not a house.

Interest to be conveyed or granted

If the dwelling-house is a house rather than a flat and the landlord owns the freehold of it, the tenant can buy the freehold. The conveyance must be of an estate in fee simple absolute, more colloquially known as freehold (HA 1985, Sched 6, para 9). If the landlord of the house does not own the freehold, but rather has a lease, provided that lease is of sufficient length the tenant is entitled to acquire a lease.

If the dwelling-house is a flat (i.e. anything other than a house), the tenant can only buy the leasehold. This is true even if the landlord has the freehold. If the landlord only has a lease, that lease must have sufficient length.

Length of lease

The length of the term which is granted is calculated in accordance with paragraph 12 of Schedule 6 to HA 1985, and depends on the landlord's own interest in the property. If the landlord is the freeholder or has a lease for an unexpired period of at least 125 years and five days, the grant must be for a term of not less than 125 years. If the landlord's interest is shorter, the grant will be for a period ending five days before the expiry of the landlord's term. So, for example, where the landlord has an unexpired lease of 80 years, the lease granted to the tenant will be for 79 years and 360 days.

Where there is more than one leasehold interest in the dwelling-house, the expiry of the shortest term is used to determine the term of the grant.

Exception for blocks of flats

There is an exception to these rules if the dwelling-house is a flat in a block where the landlord has already granted a lease under these provisions (since 8 August 1980). In these circumstances the landlord has discretion to grant a lease for a term which matches those of the other lease or leases. This aids management of the block in the future by ensuring that there are concurrent terms on all the flats.

4.
Procedure

Service of notices / Mistakes in notices /
Basic procedure / Landlord's costs /
Tenant's notice / Landlord's reply /
Tenant's notice of intention /
Completion / Registration of title /
Dealing with procedural delays

The Housing Act 1985 sets out in some detail the procedure for exercising the right to buy. The exercise proceeds through a series of notices served by the tenant and landlord. Under section 176 the Secretary of State has the power to prescribe forms to be used for each notice which has to be served. Where there is a form prescribed, the form, or one "substantially to the like effect", must be used. The current forms are contained in the Housing (Right to Buy) (Prescribed Forms) Regulations 1994 (SI No 2194), which have subsequently been amended to take into account the change to rent to mortgage and some other changes. In addition notices relating to the delay procedure are prescribed by the Housing (Right to Buy Delay Procedure) (Prescribed Forms) Regulations 1989 (SI No 240). Not all stages of the process, however, have a prescribed form. Where a form is available it is referred to by its number in the regulations (e.g. RTB 1). Forms are available in Welsh; the latest regulations at the time of writing are Housing (Right to Buy) (Prescribed Forms) (Welsh Forms) Regulations 1994 (SI No 2931). The landlord should be sure that the forms comply with the latest regulations.

Service of notices

Notice may be served by the tenant by sending it in the post (HA 1985, s 176(3)). Service will be effective at the time at which the letter would be delivered in the ordinary course of post. This means that the date on the notice is not necessarily the date of the claim or the "relevant time". The High Court Practice is that service is deemed to be effected:

1. in the case of first class mail, on the second working day after posting, and
2. in the case of second class mail, on the fourth working day after posting.

Because the time of service is important (e.g. the relevant time for the date of valuation), the actual date of service is used if there is evidence that service did not take place on the deemed date (e.g. *Maltglade v St Albans Rural District Council* [1972] 2 All ER 129).

Thus even where a tenant can show that a notice was properly addressed and posted, it is open to the authority to show that it was received much later than the second working day after posting, for example by producing a letter stamped on arrival at the office. It is the time that the notice arrives at either the authority's principal office or specified office (see below) which counts, not the time it arrives at the correct section or at the desk of the person dealing with applications. It is also open to the authority to show that it was not received at all, although this is almost impossible to prove.

Place of service

Landlords

Where the landlord is a local authority, the tenant must address the notice to the local authority and leave it at, or send it by post to, the principal office or any other office as specified by them as one where they accept right to buy applications (Local Government Act (LGA) 1972, s 231). If the landlord is a housing association the notice can be sent to the principal office or the office with which the tenant usually deals (HA 1985, s 176(4)).

Tenants

Service of any document by a local authority on a tenant may be by post (LGA 1972, s 233).

Mistakes in notices

If the tenant makes a mistake or does not provide all required particulars, the notice is not necessarily invalid. If the mistake or omission is immaterial it can be ignored. If important information is missing the landlord must ask for more details. If a mistake is discovered and as a result the wrong decision is made by the landlord on any matter, the tenant should not be penalised. The landlord may have to ask the tenant to amend, withdraw or reserve the notice (HA 1985, s 177(2) as amended) and may extend any relevant period to make sure that all parties are, as nearly as may be, in the same position as they would have been if the mistake had not been made.

   Where there is a defect in a notice, the test of whether the notice is valid is objective. The burden of proof is on the notifier to establish validity. So where a council served a notice referring to the Housing Act 1985, when in fact the claim had been made under the Housing Act 1980, the notice was held to be valid because on an objective test the recipient of the notice would not be misled. The provisions in the 1980 Act regarding that notice were almost identical (*Milne-Berry and Madden v Tower Hamlets London Borough Council* (1995) 28 HLR 225).

Basic procedure

The procedure for exercising the right to buy is contained in
Part V of the 1985 Act. Broadly speaking there are four stages
before completion.

Action by	Notice	Effect
1. Tenant	section 122 (form RTB 1)	Claim of RTB
2. Landlord	section 124 (form RTB 2)	Acceptance or rejection of RTB claim
3. Landlord	section 125	Details of proposed terms
4. Tenant	section 125D	Tenant's acceptance or rejection of terms or claim for rent to mortgage

If the tenant accepts the terms of the offer from the landlord,
the landlord is under a duty to complete; this is enforceable
by injunction. The procedure can, however, become more
complex if there are delays, either by the landlord or tenant,
or if the tenant claims the right to buy or rent to mortgage
terms. There may be dispute about whether repairs need to
be carried out, or compensation paid for improvements.
Regulations may entitle the tenant to compensation, when
his or her tenancy ends, for an improvement carried out
by the tenant or a predecessor (e.g. Secure Tenants of
Local Authorities (Compensation for Improvements)
Regulations 1994).

Landlord's costs

The landlord must bear his own costs. This includes all
costs connected with the exercise of the right to buy
(HA 1985, s 178, as substituted). For claims made before
11 October 1993 the landlord was permitted to recover from

the tenant the costs of a mortgage (up to a prescribed limit). Any agreement to pay costs is void.

Tenant's notice (form RTB 1)

The secure tenant or joint tenants must serve a written notice on the landlord claiming the right to buy (HA 1985, s 122). If the tenant requests form RTB 1 the landlord must supply it to him or her within seven days of the request (HA 1985, s 176(2)).

   If the tenant changes his or her mind at any stage right up to completion, he or she can revoke the notice in writing (HA 1985, s 122(3)). Although the Act makes no specific provision, it may be presumed that a revocation from one joint tenant does not affect the claim of the remaining tenant or tenants.

Family members

If the tenant wishes to share the right to buy with his or her family, he or she must nominate the family members in the section 122 notice (HA 1985, s 123). Any named family members who qualify under section 123 are treated for right to buy purposes as joint tenants.

Extended right to buy

If the landlord is a leaseholder and the extended right to buy provisions apply (see Chapter 9) the tenant's notice must be passed on to the superior landlord. The detailed procedure is set out in pp 123-128 below.

Landlord's reply

The landlord must respond to the tenant's notice with two notices. The first states whether the right has been accepted or denied; the second sets out the terms of the offer, if there has been acceptance (HA 1985, s 124).

Landlord's acceptance or denial (form RTB 2)

The landlord must decide whether the tenant has a right to buy and must reply by written notice served on the tenant within four weeks (HA 1985, s 124). This period is extended to eight weeks if the tenant has not spent all of his or her "qualifying period" (see Chapter 2) with that landlord. The notice may have to be amended or re-served in some circumstances where there is a change of landlord or tenant (HA 1985, ss 137, 138).

Where a section 122 notice is invalid (either because it is served by a non-secure tenant or it has been withdrawn), it appears there is no requirement to serve a section 124 notice in response. However, it is advisable in these circumstances to serve a section 124 notice denying the right to buy.

The landlord's decision must be based on the facts, and not on opinion. The tenant can challenge any denial by an action in the county court under section 181. Where there are areas of doubt (e.g. whether family members who are to be added fulfil the statutory requirement), the landlord may accept evidence in the form of a statutory declaration (HA 1985, s 180). A statutory declaration is made before a magistrate or a commissioner for oaths in a prescribed form. A false statutory declaration constitutes an act of perjury.

Only two decisions can be made: either the right is admitted or it is denied. If admitted, no reasons need be given for the decision. If denied, reasons must be given in the notice (HA 1985, s 124(1)(b)). For example, the dwelling may be exempted from the right to buy, or the tenant may not satisfy the qualifying period.

Landlord's offer notice

Where the right to buy is admitted, the landlord must then

serve a section 125 notice of terms of offer. The notice must be served within eight weeks if the landlord has admitted the right to the freehold, or 12 weeks if the landlord has admitted the right to buy a leasehold interest.

The offer notice must:

1. describe the dwelling-house;

2. state the purchase price at which, in the landlord's opinion, the tenant is entitled to buy, giving a calculation of how the price was arrived at, including:

(a) the value at the time of service of the tenant's notice claiming the right to buy, informing the tenant of his or her right under section 128 to have the value determined or re-determined by the district valuer;

(b) the improvements which can be disregarded;

(c) the discount, stating the period to be taken into account – any reductions for previous discounts or limits on the amount of discount should be stated;

3. state the provisions which the landlord considers ought to be contained in the conveyance or grant;

4. give the tenant estimates for and information on service charges and improvement contributions, if there is to be any covenant in the conveyance or grant imposing liability for these charges and contributions (see HA 1985, ss 125A, 125B; see also Chapter 6 for further discussion);

5. describe any structural defect known to the landlord affecting the dwelling-house or the building in which it is situated or any other building over which the tenant will have rights under the conveyance or lease (e.g. rights of way) (HA 1985, s 125(4A);

6. state the effect of sections 125D and 125E(1) and (4) (tenant's notice of intention, landlord's notice in default and effect of failure to comply);

7. state the effect of section 136(2) (change of tenant after service of the section 125 notice);

8. state the effect of sections 140 and 141(1), (2) and (4) (landlord's notices to complete and effect of failure to comply);

9. state the effect of the provisions relating to the right to acquire on rent to mortgage terms and the relevant amount and multipliers as determined by the Secretary of State (HA 1985, s 143 *et seq*).

Structural defect

There is no definition of structural defect. In cases on repairing covenants, structure usually means the parts of the building which are essential to its physical integrity. This means more than simply the load-bearing elements (e.g. the walls, roof and foundations), and includes other parts of the fabric, but not decorative items (see e.g. *Pearlman v Harrow School* [1979] 1 All ER 356). For example, windows have been held to be part of the structure only if they are a substantial and integral part of the wall *(Boswell v Crucible Steel Co of America* [1925] 1 KB 119). Structural defects include not only structures which have fallen into disrepair but also defective construction. There is no specific statutory remedy for failure to disclose such a defect but, given this, it is likely that an action could be taken in tort for breach of the duty to disclose, and damages awarded for any loss of value due to the defect.

Duty of care

One question which has arisen is whether serving a section 125 notice creates some duty of care on the landlord, which can lead to a claim in damages.

Case report

Mr Blake and Mr Brooks were both tenants who had bought their homes from the council on the basis of the valuation contained in the section 125 notice. They sought to argue that the council had negligently overvalued the properties and should therefore pay them damages for owning properties which were now worth less than they had paid for them. The judge rejected the argument and

> held section 125 imposed no statutory duty on the local
> authority. It was merely provided for a step in the com-
> pulsory sale transaction and for the landlord to give his
> opinion of the price at which he would sell. *Blake v Barking
> and Dagenham London Borough Council* (1996) *The Times,*
> 11 November.

Given the mechanism for appealing against the valuation
(see p 59 below) this decision is not perhaps very surprising.
Tenants who are unhappy with the valuation should use this
mechanism to challenge it.

Tenant's notice of intention

Under section 125D the tenant has a period of time to
respond to the landlord's section 125 notice. The tenant has
three choices: pursuing his or her claim; withdrawing it; or
seeking to acquire on rent to mortgage terms.

   The tenant is required to serve his or her notice of
intention within the specified period. This is 12 weeks after
service of the section 125 notice or, if it is later, 12 weeks after
receiving a section 128(5) notice (determination or re-determination by the district valuer). This period cannot be
extended other than under section 125E.

Proceeding with the claim

If the tenant wishes to proceed, he or she must serve notice
of his or her intention to continue to exercise the right to buy.
Section 125D appears not to require the tenant to agree all the
terms at this stage but merely to state whether he or she still
wishes to proceed. However, on this interpretation the section would have little practical effect and it is suggested that
the tenant must indicate whether he or she intends to proceed on the terms offered.

Withdrawing the claim

If the tenant decides to withdraw he or she must serve written notice on the landlord.

Seeking rent to mortgage terms

If the tenant decides to acquire on rent to mortgage terms his or her notice must contain the information specified in section 144.

Completion

Once the terms proposed in the section are agreed the landlord has a duty to complete (HA 1985, s 138). All four steps in the process must have been performed, i.e. the tenant must have claimed the right to buy, the right must have been established, and terms must have been proposed and agreed. The duty to complete is enforceable by injunction (HA 1985, s 138(3); see also Chapter 7) so long as the tenant remains a secure tenant *(Bradford City Metropolitan Council v McMahon* (1993) 25 HLR 534).

 If the tenant has failed to pay rent or any other payment due from him as a tenant for four weeks after it has been lawfully demanded from him the landlord is not bound to comply with section 138 while the whole or part of that payment remains outstanding (HA 1985, s 138(2)). Whether rent is due is usually a straightforward matter, but it can sometimes be more complex, for example where the tenant is claiming to withhold rent because of disrepair, or where there are arrears of housing benefit owing to the account. Where completion is refused because of apparent arrears on the account, care should be taken to assess whether these genuinely amount to rent which is due.

Status of other occupiers on completion

The secure tenancy ends on the transfer of the interest. If the secure tenant had subtenants (see C Hunter, *Tenants' Rights* (Arden's Housing Library) 1995 Chapter 3 on the rights of a secure tenant to sublet), the subtenant's interest survives the transfer under section 139(2) of HA 1985 and section 139 of the Law of Property Act 1925. A joint tenant who did not exercise the right to buy probably becomes a licensee of the new owner or leaseholder.

Registration of title

Registering title is a matter of conveyancing practice in accordance with the 1985 Act provisions.

Within two months of the conveyance or grant, registration must be applied for, if the landlord's title has not already been registered. Registration under section 123 of the Land Registration Act 1925 is compulsory (HA 1985, s 154). If the interest is a leasehold, registration must be in accordance with section 8 of the Land Registration Act 1925. This is so even if the title would not otherwise have to be registered (e.g. because it is a short lease). In practice most leases are likely to be long because of the exception to the right to buy if the landlord does not have sufficient interest (HA 1985, Sched 5, para 4). The appropriate term which must be granted is either 125 years or five days before the landlord's lease expires (HA 1985, Sched 6, para 12), but short leases may be granted under paragraph 12(3) of Schedule 6. Where the landlord's leasehold interest has already been registered, the grant to the tenant must be registered in accordance with section 22 of the Land Registration Act 1925.

Instead of requiring the usual affidavit under the Land Registration Act 1925, s 14(1), the Chief Land Registrar will accept and sign a certificate supplied by the landlord to the tenant containing the information stated in sections 154(2) and (3) – that the landlord is entitled to convey the freehold or make the grant subject only to such incumbrances, rights and interests as are stated in the conveyance or grant or summarised in the certificate. If the interest is a leasehold the certificate must give full particulars of the title of the lease and each superior title, including the title number if registered, or state whether it was investigated in the usual way on the grant of the landlord's lease. The form of the certificate must be approved by the Chief Land Registrar.

The Chief Land Registrar must, for the purpose of the registration of title, accept such a certificate as sufficient evidence of the facts stated in it; but if as a result a claim is made, the landlord is liable to indemnify the Registrar.

Dealing with procedural delays

A fairly tight timetable is set out for the process to be completed. There may be delays by either side. Those by landlords have received publicity and led to the tightening of procedures in 1988. Tenants' delays have received less publicity, but the government recognised that these could cause management problems for landlords, and in 1993 added the requirement of the tenant's notice of intention, and the penalties for failure to serve it.

Delay by tenant

Delays by the tenant may occur at one of two stages: in serving the tenant's notice of intention or in agreeing the terms of the sale and completing.

Failure to serve notice of intention

If the tenant fails to serve notice of intention within the period specified in section 125D(2), he or she does not automatically lose the right to buy. The tenant has at least

28 days' grace. He or she must first be warned, by a section 125E notice of default, that if there is no response within 28 days from the service of the section 125E notice he or she will be deemed to have withdrawn the claim. The landlord cannot serve a section 125E notice until the period specified in section 125D(2) has elapsed. Once the time (including any extended time) in the section 125E notice has expired the notice claiming to exercise the right to buy is deemed to have been withdrawn (HA 1985, s 125E(4)).

Voluntary extension of time   If the landlord wishes to extend the period of 28 days for compliance this can be done by serving written notice on the tenant before the 28 days has elapsed. There is no limit to the amount of time or the number of extensions so long as notice is served before the extended period has elapsed (HA 1985, s 125E(2)).

Mandatory extension of time   There is further provision for the compulsory extension of time under section 125E(3) before the period (or any extended period) has elapsed if "the circumstances are such that it would not be reasonable to expect the tenant to comply". The landlord must extend the period "until 28 days after the time when those circumstances no longer obtain". The consideration of reasonableness and of whether the circumstances "no longer obtain" is an objective one, rather than simply a matter for the landlord. There is no requirement on the tenant to notify the landlord of the circumstances. There may be circumstances where the landlord encounters silence from the tenant and deems the application to be withdrawn; however, the landlord may have to revive the application because, for example, the tenant was in hospital.

Failure to complete

Where the tenant has served a notice of intention to pursue his or her claim, but will not agree to all the section 125 notice or rent to mortgage terms, or indeed fails to complete following agreement, the landlord may start the two-stage "notice to complete" procedure.

First notice to complete   If the tenant fails to complete or agree to the terms within 12 months from the date of service of the landlord's section 125 notice, the landlord may serve a notice to complete under section 140. If the tenant claims the right to acquire on rent to mortgage terms, the period is 12 months from the date of service of the section 146 notice admitting or denying the right.

A section 140 notice can only be served where there has been a failure by the tenant to agree terms; therefore the landlord cannot serve a section 140 notice (HA 1985, s 140(4)):

- if the district valuer has not yet determined a value (and is required to do so);
- if there is a procedure for determining any other matter relating to the terms of the sale (e.g. details of the lease, which has not been concluded); disputes may be referred to the county court (see Chapter 7) and while any such case is pending the landlord cannot serve a section 140 notice;
- if the tenant has already served a notice on the landlord about any matter relevant to the grant and that matter has not yet been agreed in writing.

In these circumstances, either procedures are being undertaken which should lead to an agreement, or the landlord has been informed of the matter in dispute and needs to respond to the tenant's position.

The section 140 notice requires the tenant to complete within the period stated or, if there are matters which have not yet been agreed or determined, to state what those matters are. This period must be at least 56 days. The period must be "reasonable in the circumstances" and landlords must consider in each case whether a longer period is appropriate. The notice must explain to the tenant the effects of sections 140 and 141.

The service of a notice to complete is discretionary. If the tenant fails to respond to the section 140 notice, the landlord may do nothing, or may serve a second notice to complete (HA 1985, s 141).

Second notice to complete   The landlord may serve a second notice any time after the period stated in the section 140 notice has expired. The second notice requires the tenant to complete within a period stated in the notice. Again this period must be at least 56 days and must be "reasonable in the circumstances".

The second notice must inform the tenant of the effect of section 141, which is that if the tenant fails to comply with the notice, his or her claim is deemed to be withdrawn at the end of the period. The notice must also state that the landlord may extend the period before it ends (by written notice served on the tenant), in which case the claim is deemed to be withdrawn at the end of the extended period.

If, after service of the section 141 notice, the tenant fails to pay the rent due, the landlord is not bound to complete (HA 1985, s 138(2)). In these circumstances, the tenant's failure to pay rent results in the tenant being treated as if he or she had not complied with the section 141 notice. If the tenant does not comply with the notice by the end of the specified period his or her claim is deemed to be withdrawn.

If, after service of the section 141 notice (or the earlier section 140 notice), the tenant decides to claim the right to acquire on rent to mortgage terms by serving a section 144 notice, the notice to complete is automatically cancelled and no further notice to complete may be served whilst the claim remains outstanding.

Service of a section 141 notice is discretionary. If the tenant fails to comply with the notice, the landlord may decide not to rely on its notice, and not to treat the claim as withdrawn. The landlord may even be estopped from relying on its notice or it may waive the notice.

Case report

There was a defect in a notice to complete served by Tower Hamlets LBC. The tenants pointed out the invalidity of the notice and contended that there were matters which had not been agreed regarding repairs. Shortly before expiry of the notice, a council officer told the tenants' solicitor on the telephone that they would treat the right to buy application as proceeding. The court held that by the telephone conversation the council had given a clear and unqualified undertaking that the right to buy would proceed, and that the words amounted to a waiver of the notices by election. *Milne-Berry and Madden v Tower Hamlets London Borough Council* (1995) 28 HLR 225.

Delay by landlord

In certain circumstances where there is delay on the landlord's part, the tenant may serve "notice of delay". There are two notices which may be served: the "initial notice" and the "operative notice".

Initial notice of delay (form RTB 6)

The circumstances in which the initial notice may be served are where:

1. the landlord fails to serve before the appropriate time limit the section 124 notice after the right has been claimed; or

2. the landlord fails to serve before the appropriate time limit the section 125 notice after the right has been established; or

3. the tenant considers that delays on the part of the landlord are preventing him or her from exercising expeditiously:

(a) his or her right to buy; or

(b) his or her right to acquire on rent to mortgage terms (if applicable) (HA 1985, s 153A).

The initial notice must specify:

    i) the circumstances in which the notice is served (**1.–3.** above);

    ii) the most recent action of which the tenant is aware which has been taken by the landlord as part of the procedure;

    iii) a response period; the tenant can choose how much time to give the landlord to respond but he or she must allow at least a month. Time runs from the date of service of the notice.

The tenant can serve further initial notices if there are further delays (HA 1985, s 153A(6)).

Counter notice (form RTB 7)

The landlord responds to the initial notice by service of a counter notice, which may be served if:

    1. the complaint is about failure to serve the section 124 or 125 notice and the landlord has already served the appropriate notice, or is able to serve it with the counter notice; or

    2. the complaint is about some other delay (see item **3.** under "Initial notice of delay", above) and the landlord has taken whatever action needed to be taken to allow expeditious completion of the right to buy (HA 1985, s 153A(3)).

The reason for serving the counter notice must be stated in the notice. A counter notice may be appropriate where, for example, there is a dispute regarding the terms of the conveyance or lease, and the tenant is refusing to agree. The tenant may argue that the terms being proposed are unreasonable. In *Guinan v Enfield London Borough Council* (1996) 29 HLR 456, the Court of Appeal held that a counter notice is valid if the landlord in good faith believes that he has in law the right to insist upon the terms that he is offering. At that point he can validly say that there is no further action to be taken.

If the counter notice is served within the response time, the initial notice of delay is automatically cancelled. There is nothing to stop the tenant serving further initial notices if the appropriate circumstances arise again.

Operative notice of delay (form RTB 8)

If the counter notice is not served within the response time, or not served at all, the tenant may then serve an "operative notice of delay" under section 153B. In summary, the effect of this notice is that the landlord must treat any rent payments after a specified date as payment on account towards the purchase price or initial payment.

The specified date, which must be given in the operative notice of delay, depends upon the circumstances in which the initial notice of delay was served. If the complaint was about failure to serve the section 124 or 125 notice, the specified date is the default date (i.e. the date by which the notice should have been served). If the complaint was about some other delay, the specified date is the date of service of the notice.

Once the operative notice of delay has been served, rent payments (but not rates, council tax or service charges) over a certain period must be treated not only as payment of rent but also as payment on account. That period starts with the specified date (see above) and ends with the earliest of the following dates:

- service of the counter notice;
- completion;

- withdrawal or deemed withdrawal of the tenant's right to buy claim;
- when the tenant ceases to be entitled to exercise the right to buy (HA 1985, s 153B).

The payment reduces the purchase price or the tenant's initial payment (towards acquisition on rent to mortgage terms). See Chapter 5 for the calculation of the purchase price.

The service of an operative notice of delay may affect repayment of discount provisions.

5.
The Price and Paying It

Value of dwelling-house / Disputes about
valuation / The discount / Paying for
the property / Right to acquire on rent
to mortgage terms

The amount which the tenant has to pay for the property
is its value less any applicable discount (HA 1985, s 126).
If tenants had to pay full value for the properties the right
to buy would undoubtedly have been far less popular. The
discount, whether seen as an inducement to leave the
public sector or as a recognition of the secure tenancy's
value, has put the price of home ownership within the range
of many tenants.

Value of dwelling-house

The first stage in arriving at the price is the calculation of the
value. The valuation is made at the "relevant time" (i.e. the
date on which the tenant's notice of claim is served). The
value is the price which the dwelling-house would realise
if sold on the open market by a willing vendor and after
making certain assumptions (HA 1985, s 127).

Who should conduct the valuation?

The landlord may choose any person to conduct the valuation. The district valuer has a role to play in resolving dis-

putes about valuation (see below) but this does not mean
that he or she cannot also carry out the initial valuation.

Case report

In the early 1980s there were complaints made by tenants
exercising the right to buy under the Housing Act 1980
that Norwich City Council took too long to make the initial price valuation. The Secretary of State intervened but
the council objected and took the matter to court. The
Court of Appeal decided that it was in no way unjust or
improper for the council to use the district valuer or one
of the district valuer's junior staff even though the district
valuer has a quasi-judicial role when it comes to dealing
with disputes.

There were also complaints that the council
caused delay generally and by insisting on large scale maps
and on pre-purchase "counselling" interviews. The
Secretary of State's decision that the "tenants have or may
have difficulty in exercising the right to buy effectively and
expeditiously" was upheld. The council's failure to use the
district valuer for initial valuations was blamed for the
main burden of complaints. Lord Denning approved of the
following practice: a person in the district valuer's office
prepares the "draft" valuation, and if the tenant objects
then someone else in the office – the valuation officer or
his deputy – revises the valuation. It was said by Lord
Denning that "no tenant has ever complained" of the
system. *R v Secretary of State for the Environment, ex p
Norwich City Council* [1982] QB 808, [1982] 1 AER 737).

The landlord does not owe a duty of care which could
found an action in tort in carrying out the valuation (*Blake v
Barking and Dagenham London Borough Council* (1996) *The
Times*, 11 November).

Valuation assumptions

There are assumptions which must be made in preparing the
valuation as specified in section 127, which should be
referred to for its detailed provisions.

Disregard of improvements or internal disrepair

Any improvements made by persons specified in section 127(4) must be disregarded (HA 1985, s 127(1)(b). Any such improvements should have received consent from the council (for definition of improvement, which includes, for example, external decoration see A Kilpatrick, *Repairs and Maintenance* (Arden's Housing Library) 1996, Chapter 9).

Case report

A tenant carried out works which he said were improvements which increased the property's value but were to be disregarded. The property when he moved into it was in a poor state, and he carried out a large number of unconnected works on it. The county court held that the works should be classified as "repairs", not "improvements", and should not be disregarded for valuation purposes. The Court of Appeal upheld the decision that the works were not so extensive that they went beyond mere repair and renewal, and held that the word "improvements" had the specific meaning given to it by section 187. The Court of Appeal said that the judge was obliged to examine each and every item singly to determine whether they were repairs or improvements. *Dickinson v Enfield London Borough Council* (1996) 29 HLR 465, CA.

Any failure by any of the specified persons to keep the dwelling-house in good internal repair must also be disregarded. In other words in general the surveyor must attempt a valuation of the property as if it were maintained by the tenant according to the tenancy agreement in the condition it was in when the tenancy began.

The persons specified in section 127(4) are:

1. The secure tenant him- or herself.

2. Any of the tenant's predecessors in the same tenancy. A tenancy remains the same tenancy when there is

a succession or valid assignment or where a joint tenant joins or leaves the tenancy. Although all assignments preserve the tenancy, persons who assigned their tenancy by way of exchange under section 92 are specifically excluded by section 127(4). Sometimes it appears that on a transfer, the tenancy is the same tenancy when in fact a new tenancy is created (for examples of case-law on this subject, see C Hunter, *Tenants' Rights* (Arden's Housing Library) 1995, Chapter 2). Where there is a new tenancy, any improvements or dilapidation caused by the previous tenant must be taken into account in valuing the property (unless the previous tenant is a family member, see below). Careful enquiries about the history of the tenancy should be made before disregarding any improvements made by previous tenants.

    3. Any member of the tenant's family who, immediately before the secure tenancy was granted, was a secure tenant of the same dwelling-house under another tenancy. In this case it does not matter whether there was a valid assignment or succession or the creation of a new tenancy. It appears that the person must be a member of the tenant's family at the time of valuation, but need not have been so under the previous tenancy.

Any failure by the landlord to comply with its duty to repair decreases the value; any improvements by the landlord raise the value. The same applies to any previous landlords, non-secure tenants under previous tenancies or other persons who do not fall within section 127(4).

Service charges and improvement contributions

The valuation must be made on the assumption that the amount of service charges or improvement contributions is at least the same as the estimate given in the section 125 notice (HA 1985, s 127(1)(c)).

Vacant possession

Where the freehold is being sold, the assumption is that the vendor is selling for an estate in fee simple with vacant possession. Where there is sale of the leasehold, that lease is granted with vacant possession for the appropriate termwhich is usually 125 years and with a ground rent not exceeding £10 per annum.

No existing interest in purchase

Where the buyer is known to be particularly interested, this may increase value. Therefore the assumption is made that neither the tenant nor a family member residing with him or her wanted to buy the freehold or take the lease. This means that the valuation is made as though there is no existing interest in purchasing the property.

Terms of grant or conveyance

The final assumption is that the terms which must be included in the conveyance or grant by virtue of the Housing Act 1985 are actually included (see Chapter 6 below).

Reduction for operative notice of delay

Where an operative notice of delay has been served, the purchase price or initial payment is reduced by the total payments made during the delay period calculated in accordance with section 153B(1). If this period is more than a year, a bonus of 50 per cent of the total payments must be credited to the tenant's account.

Disputes about valuation

Any question over the value must be determined by the district valuer in accordance with section 128. With any other type of dispute (e.g. about the entitlement to a discount) the tenant can apply to the county court for a declaration or other remedy; however disputes about valuation are outside that court's jurisdiction under section 181.

Determination

If the tenant is not happy with the valuation given in the section 125 notice he or she may require a determination by serving a notice on the landlord under section 128(2). At present no standard form has been prescribed. Notice must be served within three months of service of the section 125 notice, or if there are proceedings between the landlord and tenant, within three months of the final determination of those proceedings. Final determination is usually defined as being the time when the period allowed for appeal against the decision or for leave to appeal has expired.

Re-determination

If the tenant is still not happy with the valuation, and the three-month period has not expired, he or she may request a further determination by serving notice on the landlord.

There is one situation in which a re-determination may take place outside the three-month period. Where after a determination has been made there are proceedings between the parties (e.g. about the land to be included in the sale, which may effect the value), a re-determination may be requested by either the landlord or the tenant within four weeks of the final determination of the case (HA 1985, s 128(3)). If the request comes from the tenant the notice must be in writing. There is no such requirement for the landlord, but if the landlord seeks a re-determination, it must notify the tenant in writing.

Procedure by district valuer

Before making a determination the district valuer must consider any representations made by the landlord or tenant provided they are made within four weeks of the tenant's or landlord's notice requesting the determination (HA 1985, s 128(4)). The same applies to a re-determination.

Challenging the district valuer

There is no statutory appeal procedure against the valuation. The Secretary of State has the power to intervene where the tenant has or may have difficulty in exercising effectively and expeditiously the right to buy (HA 1985, s 164); but this does not appear to include disputes about valuations. If the district valuer fails to act judicially and in accordance with natural justice his decision may be subject to judicial review.

Procedure following determination

Once a determination or re-determination has been made the landlord must "as soon as practicable" serve a notice on the tenant (HA 1985, s 128(5)). The notice must contain the effect of the determination and, even if some matters remain unchanged, must also contain:

    1. a description of the dwelling-house;
    2. the price at which, in the landlord's opinion, the tenant is entitled to buy;
    3. a calculation of how the price was arrived at including:
    (a) the value at the time of service of the tenant's notice claiming the right to buy;
    (b) any improvements which are disregarded;
    (c) the discount, stating the period to be taken into account, and any reductions for previous discounts or limits on the amount of discount where applicable;

4. the provisions which the landlord considers ought to be contained in the conveyance or grant (HA 1985, s 125).

The discount

Every person who exercises the right to buy is entitled to a discount (HA 1985, s 129). The amount of the discount is calculated in accordance with section 129(2) of Schedule 4 to HA 1985. The discount may have to be repaid if the house or flat is subsequently sold (HA 1985, s 155).

Percentage entitlement

The discount is measured as a percentage of the purchase price (i.e. the property value). The percentage increases with the length of the qualification period (though up to a maximum), and so rewards long-standing tenants with increased discounts. (See Chapter 2, which explains how the qualification period is calculated.)

Everyone who exercises the right to buy is entitled to a basic percentage. The percentages are as follows:

1. for a house, 33 per cent basic rate, increasing to a maximum of 60 per cent;

2. for a flat, 44 per cent basic rate, increasing to a maximum of 70 per cent (HA 1985, s 129(2)).

As the tenant is not entitled to exercise the right to buy until two years as a public sector tenant have elapsed, it is not until three whole years have been completed that the tenant is entitled to an increase over the basic discount. That increase is 1 per cent for each full year beyond the first two years. So for the first four years the percentages are:

Years completed	House	Flat
less than 3	33%	44%
less than 4	34%	45%
less than 5	35%	46%

As well as the percentage maximum, there are two other limits on the amount of the discount which can be made (HA 1985, s 131).

Cost floor

First, the price must not be lower than the "cost floor". This is the Secretary of State's determination of the costs (generally capital costs including major repairs) treated as incurred in respect of the dwelling-house over an eight-year period before the claim. The period starts with the beginning of the accounting period in which the eighth year falls. Costs are treated as incurred if payment was made for them during that period (for guidance on assessing such costs, see Housing (Right to Buy) (Cost Floor) Determinations 1992 and 1993).

Maximum discount

Secondly, in any event, the Secretary of State can, by order, determine a maximum discount. The discount cannot be more than this prescribed amount, even if this means a reduction on the percentage which the tenant would otherwise be entitled to. The maximum discount at the time of writing is £50,000 (Housing (Right to Buy) (Maximum Discount) Order 1989 (SI No 513)).

Entitlement to discount

The entitlement to a discount applies to any person who exercises the right to buy. Where there are joint tenants the longest qualification period is used. This also applies to family members who are treated as joint tenants by section 123.

Previous purchasers

Where purchasers have previously purchased under the right to buy and received a discount, or where their spouses have done so, there is still entitlement to a discount, but it may be reduced. Where the tenant, a joint tenant or any one of the persons exercising the right to buy has previously obtained a discount, any previous discount is deducted unless it has been paid back (HA 1985, s 130). The penalty also applies if at the time the claim is made the current or any deceased spouse of any of those persons received a previous discount (provided they were living together at the time of making the claim or at the time of death). If the right to buy was shared, only a proportion of the discount is deducted.

Example

A tenant was previously married to Mr Jones, when he exercised the right to buy and was in receipt of a discount of £8,700. Since Mr Jones's death, Mrs Jones remarried and is now living with her husband, Mr Smith, in a council house where they are joint tenants. They have now applied to exercise the right to buy. The £8,700 will be deducted from the new discount.

If Mr Jones had exercised the right to buy prior to his marriage, but jointly with his brother, only half of the discount would have to be deducted.

Where the purchase is under rent to mortgage terms, a proportionate amount to the tenant's initial payment of the previous discount has to be repaid (HA 1985, s 148).

Change of tenant

Where there is a change of tenant under section 136, the new tenant must be put in the same position as the former tenant, including the calculation of the discount, and is thus entitled to the former tenant's discount.

> *Case report*
>
> Mrs McIntyre was the daughter of a tenant of a council house. The tenant claimed the right to buy but before completion, she died and Mrs McIntyre succeeded to the tenancy. Mrs McIntyre wanted to continue with the purchase, but the council decided that she was entitled to a lesser discount. The court held that Mrs McIntyre was entitled to the same discount as her mother. *McIntyre v Merthyr Tydfil District Council* (1989) 21 HLR 320, CA.

Paying for the property

Notwithstanding the large discounts for those acquiring under the right to buy, it has been recognised in the legislation that some tenants still cannot raise sufficient capital through a mortgage from private lenders to buy the property. Accordingly different provisions were introduced, including the rights to mortgage and to purchase on shared ownership terms, to assist those at the financial margin, which are now all replaced by the right to acquire on rent to mortgage terms.

Right to acquire on rent to mortgage terms

This right was introduced by section 108 of the Leasehold Reform, Housing and Urban Development Act 1993. The scheme has been described as "an unmitigated disaster" and despite a costly publicity campaign only 13 properties were sold in the first 18 months of the scheme (*Inside Housing*,

3 November 1995). Many tenants are disqualified from the scheme because they receive housing benefit.

Essentially, the scheme turns rental payments into mortgage payments. The tenant makes an initial payment when he or she acquires the lease or freehold. The amount outstanding (the "landlord's share") must be repaid on subsequent disposal of the property or on the death of the last family member to live there. The liability to repay this amount is the mortgage on the property.

Given the limited use of the scheme, it is likely that many landlords have not encountered any claims, or at least any that have made it to completion. An outline of the scheme is set out below, but because of the rarity of its use this is limited to the statutory materials, without detailed examples.

Persons entitled to the scheme

The right belongs to a secure tenant together with either any joint tenant who also has, or a person who has been nominated to share, the right to buy. The right to buy must have been established and remain in force.

It seems that one joint tenant cannot exclude any of the other joint tenants from exercising the right to acquire on rent to mortgage terms. It is not clear how a dispute between joint tenants over this matter should be resolved. Each person wishing to acquire on rent to mortgage terms must sign the section 144 claim form. Presumably if one of the persons who has an established right to buy fails to make a section 144 claim, he or she will not lose the right to buy, but the rent to mortgage scheme will be followed.

When the right cannot be exercised

Loss of right to buy

The right goes hand in hand with the right to buy itself, so if the right to buy is lost or cannot be exercised, there is no right to acquire on rent to mortgage terms (HA 1985, s 121). Circumstances in which the right to buy cannot be exercised are described above in Chapter 2 and below in Chapter 7. These include situations in which a possession order has been granted or where there are certain bankruptcy proceedings.

Entitlement to housing benefit

The right to acquire on rent to mortgage terms cannot be exercised if the tenant was entitled to housing benefit during any part of the "relevant period".

The start of the "relevant period" is twelve months before the day on which the tenant makes his claim to exercise the right to acquire on rent to mortgage terms. The period ends with the actual conveyance or grant so the tenant should be informed of the housing benefit rules as soon as he or she makes his or her claim because he or she is not "safe" until the final step.

If the tenant has made a claim for, but has not received or been informed of a right to, housing benenfit, he or she is still excluded from the rent to mortgage scheme.

Although the Act refers to the "tenant", it is not clear whether the right is excluded if one of the other persons jointly entitled to the right to buy falls within the benefit exclusions.

Income too high

Those who are able to finance the purchase themselves from raising a mortgage conventionally are also excluded from the right. This is achieved by calculating minimum and maximum initial payments. Calculation is made of a hypothetical mortgage based on current payments of rent. If that hypothetical capital borrowing (the "minimum initial payment") exceeds the maximum initial payment (see below), the right is not available (HA 1985, s 143B).

The maximum initial payment   This is 80 per cent of the price which would be payable if the tenant were exercising the right to buy.

A calculation of the price of the dwelling-house must be made in accordance with the provisions of section 126. The price is the value less any discount. The tenant may request a determination by the district valuer of the value being used for this purpose.

The minimum initial payment   For a house, there are two different formulae. P is the minimum initial payment in each case. The choice of formula depends upon whether the weekly rent on the house exceeds "the relevant amount", which is determined by the Secretary of State. Since 1 September 1996 this has been £44.45, but the amount may be varied. The Secretary of State gives his determination by a declaration rather than an order (the most recent declaration at the time of writing is the Housing (Rent to Mortgage) (Multipliers and Relevant Amount) Declaration 1996).

The Secretary of State also determines two figures which are used in both the formulae below. Those figures are both called "the multiplier" but they are different for each formula.

If the weekly rent (at the time of service of the landlord's section 146 notice) did not exceed the relevant amount (i.e. was £44.45 or less), the formula is:

$$P = R \times M$$

where   R =   the weekly rent
        M =   the multiplier (674.90 at the time of writing)

If the weekly rent did exceed the relevant amount (i.e. was more than £44.45), the formula is:

$$P = Q + (E \times M)$$

where   Q = the qualifying maximum for the year during which the section 146 notice was served (see Income and Corporation Taxes Act 1988, s 367(5). The qualifying maximum at the time of writing is £30,000)

E = the amount by which the weekly rent exceeded the relevant amount

M = the multiplier (613.12 at the time of writing)

For a flat, the same calculations have to be made using the relevant formula, as if the flat were a house. The minimum initial payment is then reduced to 80 per cent of that calculation.

Procedure

As with other elements of the right to buy, the procedure involves the serving of notices and counter notices.

The claim

The tenant must serve a section 144 notice on the landlord (form RTB 3) (Housing (Right to Buy) (Prescribed Forms) Regulations 1986 (SI No 2194)). This form, or one "substantially to the like effect", must be used to make a claim.

The application is made on behalf of the tenant and all other persons claiming the right. If the right is exercised at a late stage (i.e. after the landlord has served one of the notices to complete), the section 144 claim cancels the notice to complete and the landlord cannot serve another whilst the claim to acquire on rent to mortgage terms is outstanding.

Landlord's reply

The landlord must "as soon as practicable" serve on the tenant (unless the claim has been withdrawn) a section 146 notice admitting or denying the right (form RTB 3A). If the right is denied, the landlord must give reasons. If the right is admitted, two amounts must be ascertained by the landlord:

(a) the landlord's residual liability (the "landlord's share"), and

(b) the initial discount given to the tenant (HA 1985, s 148).

These calculations must be done twice. The first is on the basis of the minimum initial payment. The tenant then proposes the initial payment he is prepared to make and the calculations must be re-done on the basis of that initial payment.

The landlord must give the tenant the following information:

1. The "minimum initial payment" and two of the figures used in its calculation (i.e. the "relevant amount" and the "multipliers"). It seems that the dwelling-house's value does not have to be given. It is therefore difficult for the tenant to challenge the valuation.

2. The proportion which the minimum initial payment bears to the price (which would be payable if the tenant exercised the right to buy).

3. The landlord's share on the assumption that the tenant makes the minimum initial payment. The landlord's share, a percentage, is determined by the formula:

$$\frac{P - IP}{P} \times 100$$

where   P =   the price (if the right to buy were exercised)

IP =   the initial payment.

4. The amount of the initial discount on that assumption. The initial discount is determined by the formula:

$$\frac{IP}{P} \times D$$

where   D =   the discount (if the right to buy were being exercised).

5. The provisions which, in the landlord's opinion, should be contained in the conveyance or grant and the mortgage required by section 151B including provisions for the redemption of the landlord's share.

Tenant's notice of intention

The tenant must then decide what to do about his or her claim and within 12 weeks from service of the landlord's section 146 notice (RTB 3A) must serve a notice of intention. There is no prescribed form for the notice but it must state either that he or she:

1. intends to pursue the claim; or
2. withdraws the claim and intends to pursue the claim to exercise the right to buy; or
3. withdraws both of these claims.

If under **1.** above the tenant intends to pursue the claim, he or she must state the amount of the initial payment he or she proposes to make. This must be not less than the minimum and not more than the maximum initial payment quoted in the RTB 3A. The tenant can change his or her mind about the amount and notify the landlord at any time before completion by notice in writing.

Notice of terms

If the tenant notifies the landlord of his or her intention to proceed, the landlord must "as soon as practicable" serve a section 147 notice. The tenant will have stated what amount he or she is prepared to pay for the initial payment. The landlord must then re-calculate and state the amounts for the "landlord's share" and the "initial discount" based on the tenant's figure.

The landlord has to provide the statement each time the tenant proposes a new initial payment. If the tenant notifies the landlord that he or she wishes instead to exercise the right to buy, the landlord must take whatever steps are necessary to process the claim, depending on the stage of the procedure.

Completion

If the tenant agrees with the terms and all relevant matters then the landlord has a duty to convey the freehold or grant the lease (cf HA 1985, s 139; HA 1985, s 150). The only lawful excuse for failing to comply with section 150 is if the tenant has failed to pay rent or any other payment, such as rates, due from him as a tenant for a period of four weeks after it has been lawfully demanded. The landlord must complete as soon as payment is made of the full amount (HA 1985, s 150(2)).

The liability for the redemption of the landlord's share is a mortgage on the property; a mortgage deed must be drawn up as well as a deed of conveyance or grant (HA 1985, s 151B(8)). The Secretary of State may prescribe the deed's contents, although no orders have yet been made at the time of writing. Other terms may be included if they are agreed. If there is a dispute, either party may make an application to the county court for a decision on the basis of what is "reasonably required" to be included (HA 1985, s 151B(9)).

Dealing with delay

As with other stages of the right to buy there are provisions to deal with delay by either the tenant or the landlord.

Delay by tenant   If the tenant fails to respond to the section 146 notice (form RTB 3A) within 12 weeks, the landlord may serve a notice in default under section 146B requiring him or her to serve that notice within 28 days. There is no prescribed form as yet. The 12-week period may be extended by the landlord (by written notice) before it ends. (It may be extended automatically if "the circumstances are such that it would not be reasonable to expect the tenant to comply".) The section 146B notice in default must inform the tenant of the effect of the notice, in that if the tenant fails to comply, the claim will be deemed to be withdrawn at the end of the period. Unlike the right to buy provisions the tenant has only one chance to respond. There is no prohibition against the tenant pursuing his or her claim to exercise the right to buy (provided the claim is not deemed to be withdrawn).

If the tenant delays completion, the landlord may serve notices to complete under sections 152 and 153. This part of the procedure is identical to the right to buy procedure (HA 1985, ss 140 and 141).

Delay by landlord   The tenant's notice of delay, which may be served under section 153A may be served where the tenant considers that delays on the landlord's part are preventing him or her from exercising expeditiously his or her right to acquire on rent to mortgage terms.

Withdrawal

If the tenant decides to purchase the property outright, perhaps because he or she has obtained a mortgage from a building society or bank, he or she may withdraw the claim to the right to acquire on rent to mortgage terms by serving a notice in writing on the landlord (HA 1985, s 144(2)). If the tenant wishes to withdraw altogether by withdrawing the section 122 notice he or she automatically loses the right to acquire on rent to mortgage terms.

Change of landlord

The provisions under section 149 are similar to those applicable to the right to buy under section 137. The tenant must be put in the same position as if the new landlord had been the landlord at the time of claim. If there are any material differences, new notices may have to be served. The right to acquire on rent to mortgage terms is lost if the right to buy is lost.

Terms in conveyance or grant

The usual terms must be included in the grant or conveyance (i.e. those listed in Schedule 6 to HA 1985. Under section 155(3) as amended, the covenant to repay the discount must be included. Where the right to acquire on rent to mortgage terms is exercised, there are additional terms which must be included. The liability for the redemption of the landlord's share, (i.e. the outstanding amount secured by the mortgage) must be discharged on certain disposals or the tenant's death. Schedule 6A requires provision for redemption of the landlord's share to be included in the grant or conveyance.

The priority of the mortgage over other mortgages in the property is determined in accordance with section 151B. The mortgage to redeem the landlord's share takes priority immediately after a mortgage from an approved lending institution, for example for a loan taken out by the tenant to pay his or her initial share. If the landlord gives consent, the mortgage to redeem the landlord's share may be postponed to another mortgage. The landlord must give consent if the mortgage is a loan for an approved purpose. These are the same as those listed in section 156.

Under Schedule 6A the conveyance or grant must contain the following covenants.

Compulsory redemption of landlord's share

The covenant binds the secure tenant and his successors in title. Liability is a charge on the property. The covenant is to make a final payment of the amount required to redeem the landlord's share. The tenant covenants to pay this amount on the occurrence of the first of the following events:

1. after the making of a "relevant disposal which is not an excluded disposal", or

2. the expiry of one year after the death of a person who, immediately before his death, was the last person to have an interest in the property; this is called a "relevant death".

"Relevant disposal" is defined in section 159. "Excluded disposal" is defined in paragraph 1(2) of Schedule 6A, and is similar to that of exempted disposals in section 160. A disposal is excluded if:

(a) one of the transferees is the same person (or one of them or the spouse of one of the persons) who makes the disposal; or

(b) the property is inherited; or

(c) it is made under certain property transfer orders.

Voluntary payments   The conveyance or grant must include the right to make a final payment to redeem the landlord's share at any time. There must also be provision for the right to make interim payments at any time. An interim payment must be for at least 10 per cent of the dwelling-house's value (HA 1985, Sched 6A, paras 2 and 6).

These rights are exercised by written notice served on the landlord which may be withdrawn at any time by written notice. In any event, the notice will be deemed to be withdrawn if the relevant assessed payment is not made within three months. There is nothing to stop a new notice being served at any time.

Valuation costs

The tenant or his or her successors must be required, by provision in the grant or conveyance, to pay the costs of an independent valuation should there be a dispute about the valuation of the property (HA 1985, Sched 6A, para 9). This

particularly harsh provision allows the landlord no discretion to waive the costs even if the valuation resolves a
dispute in the tenant's favour.

Costs of redemption

The landlord cannot charge for costs incurred in making
a final payment. Any provision attempting to do so will
be void (HA 1985, Sched 6A, para 10).

Other covenants

The test of reasonableness applies to other covenants.

Redemption of landlord's share

While the tenant is free to pay off the landlord's share
voluntarily at any time, in certain circumstances payment
is *required*. Where there is a relevant (though not excluded)
disposal or where a period of one year has elapsed after a
relevant death, the final payment becomes due.

The amount which must be repaid is calculated in
accordance with the formula:

$$\frac{V \times S}{100}$$

where   V = the value of the dwelling-house
          S = the landlord's share.

The final discount is then deducted from this amount.

The landlord's share depends on whether there has been any
interim payment. There is a complicated formula given in
paragraph 7 of Schedule 6A which takes into account the
interim discount and any previous discounts. The valuation
is made at the time of redemption. The value must be agreed

or determined in accordance with paragraph 8 of the Schedule; the value is the open market value making various assumptions and disregarding, for example, tenant's improvements. Special provision is made where the propety is damaged by fire, etc. If the parties cannot agree a valuation, an independent valuer may be brought in, but the tenant or freeholder will have to pay the cost (see above).

By paragraph 4 of Schedule 6A, the final discount is 20 per cent if the redemption is by a person or persons all of whom were the secure tenants or qualifying persons (i.e. a qualifying spouse or a qualifying resident – see the definitions in paragraph 12 of Schedule 6A). This discount may also be claimed for a period of up to two years after the secure tenant or a qualifying spouse ceases to have a beneficial interest in the property. The Secretary of State may vary the amount of the discount by order. None has been made at the time of writing.

The total purchase price for a dwelling-house cannot be established when the right to acquire on rent to mortgage terms is exercised. It is the aggregate of the initial payment, the final payment and any interim payments that are made. These payments depend on the property valuation at the time payment is made and on any discount applicable at the time. When the final payment is calculated, the final discount must not reduce the total purchase price below the amount prescribed by paragraph 5 of Schedule 6A and section 131 (i.e. £50,000).

The covenant to redeem the landlord's share and the covenant to repay the discount are charges on the property.

6.
The Grant or Conveyance

Repayment of discount / Covenants common to leasehold and freehold interests / Covenants to be included in freehold conveyances / Covenants to be included in grant of a lease / Provisions affecting future disposals

The Housing Act 1985 makes provision for terms (referred to as covenants in the legislation) to be included in the grant (of the lease) or conveyance (of the freehold). Most of these provisions are prescribed by section 139. If the freehold is to be conveyed, the conveyance must conform with Parts I and II of Schedule 6. If a lease is to be granted the grant must conform with Parts I and III of that Schedule. In some circumstances the terms are mandatory, in others they may be modified by agreement. This chapter sets out the law as it relates to current and future conveyances and grants. The law has changed on a number of occasions, and earlier conveyances and leases may be different. Conveyancing is a very technical process: a detailed discussion of this subject is beyond the scope of this book.

Repayment of discount

One of the most important terms applied to both freeholders and leaseholders is the covenant to repay the discount if the property is sold within three years of the purchase (HA 1985, s 155). The wording of the covenant depends on whether the tenant has exercised the right to buy or the right to acquire on rent to mortgage terms (see HA 1985, s 155(2) and (3)).

The covenant is to pay the discount, or part of it, to the landlord on demand if there is a relevant (though not exempted) disposal (see below) within the three-year period. If there is more than one disposal, only the first one counts. The tenant is only obliged to pay if asked to do so. A proper demand must be served. If the tenant does not pay in accordance with the covenant, the landlord may be able to sue subsequent owners. The liability to repay the discount remains a charge on the property (see below).

Relevant disposals

Most sales attract the requirement to repay the discount. The following are relevant disposals which do attract the requirement to repay (HA 1985, s 159):

1. a further conveyance of the freehold or an assignment of the lease of all or part of the dwelling-house;

2. the grant of a long lease, i.e. for a term of more than 21 years (assuming an option to renew or extend is exercised and ignoring any option to terminate) otherwise than at a rack rent (i.e. at a ground rather than full market rent). This does not include a mortgage.

Conveyance is not defined but is probably used in the wider sense of transfer of ownership of registered land. If one joint tenant releases his interest to the others there would not be a conveyance since his or her right is merely extinguished. It is not clear whether or to what extent a declaration of trust is a relevant disposal and accordingly whether these provisions could be avoided by such a mechanism.

Exempt disposals

The requirement to repay the discount does not apply where the sale is exempt (HA 1985, s 160). A relevant disposal under any of the circumstances detailed below is exempt:

1. A disposal of the whole dwelling-house to a qualifying person. If the transfer is to more than one person, they must all be qualifying persons. A qualifying person is:

(a) the person, or one of the persons, who makes the disposal;

(b) that person's spouse or former spouse;

(c) a family member (see Chapter 1) who has been residing with that person for a 12-month period ending with the disposal.

2. The whole dwelling-house is inherited by will or intestacy.

3. It is a disposal of the whole of the dwelling-house in pursuance of a court order under various matrimonial and family legislation.

4. The disposal is made under a compulsory purchase order.

5. The disposal is of land added to the original purchase by virtue of section 184.

Amount to be repaid

The amount of the discount which must be repaid depends on the period which has elapsed since the conveyance or grant. During the first year after the original purchase the full discount is payable. Thereafter the discount is reduced by one-third for each complete year which has elapsed before the date of disposal.

Rent to mortgage

The same covenant must be made where the right to acquire on rent to mortgage terms is exercised. Here the discount is that to which the tenant was entitled on making the initial payment, any interim payment or the final payment. The discount is reduced in each case as above (i.e. by one-third for each complete year which has elapsed before the disposal) (HA 1985, s 155(3)).

Calculating the three-year period

Where the right to buy is exercised, the three-year period starts with the conveyance or grant. Where the right to acquire on rent to mortgage terms is exercised, the three-year period starts when the initial payment is made; the discount repayable is the discount either on the initial payment or any further payments (reduced by the appropriate amount for each payment).

Charge on the property

The liability to repay the discount automatically becomes a charge on the property (HA 1985, s 156). It is similar to creating a mortgage on the property but there is no need for a deed. The charge is protected by entering a notice or caution on the land register.

Priority of charges

Whether the charge on the land has priority over other charges (e.g. mortgages) is an important question. The general applicability of the rules on the priority of charges is outside the scope of this book. There may be other charges which under general legal rules take priority over that which secures the liability to repay the discount. In such a case the liability to repay the discount does not bind the owner of the prior charge.

In other cases the priority of charges is as follows:

1. Where the right to buy has been exercised, the charge has priority immediately after any mortgage lent by an approved lending institution for that purpose. (The Housing (Right to Buy) (Priority of Charges) Orders regularly update the list of approved lending institutions. There were about 15 such institutions at the time of writing.)

2. Where the right to acquire on rent to mortgage terms has been exercised, there are two other charges which take priority:

(a) the charge which secures the liability to repay the discount: this has priority immediately after the mortgage which must be provided to secure redemption of the landlord's share under section 151B;

(b) the mortgage in (a) above has priority immediately after any mortgage lent by an approved lending institution for the purpose of enabling the exercise of that right.

3. In either case, other types of charges may take priority:

(a) Under section 156(2A) charges securing other loans or further advances take priority if, and only if, the landlord gives its consent by written notice served on the institution concerned. The landlord must give consent if the purpose of the advance or further advance which is secured on the charge is for an approved purpose, as stated in section 156(4A), which includes a loan to:

    i) enable the tenant to make an interim or final payment;

    ii) enable the tenant to pay the cost of works to, or of service charges or insurance payable for, the dwelling-house (this includes loans, for example, to pay for structural works to the block in which a flat is situated);

    iii) discharge any mortgage which already has priority or to discharge any arrears or costs which have arisen on that mortgage.

(b) Priority over the repayment of the discount must be *postponed* under section 156(2B) to a charge which secures a loan made by an approved lending institution to the tenant for an approved purpose (see above). The land-

lord is required to serve notice on the institution postpon-
ing the charge. Even where not for an approved purpose the
landlord *may* serve such a notice (HA 1985, s 156).

Covenants common to leasehold and freehold interests

Rights to be conveyed or granted

When purchasing any property it is important that not only
the land is conveyed but also the buildings on it, and other
related rights such as access (HA 1985, Sched 6, Pt I). In general land law this is achieved through section 62 of the Law
of Property Act 1925. By section 62 a conveyance of land is
deemed to include, and operates to convey, with the land, all
buildings, erections, fixtures, rights and easements. In some
cases these words can create new easements as well as trans-
ferring those which already exist. With minor exceptions the
words implied by section 62 cannot be excluded or restricted
unless the tenant consents.

Related rights

Rights of access to utilities and to the property should be
included in the grant or conveyance. However, this does not
necessarily give exclusive right of access. If neighbouring
properties have rights of access to utilities running through
the property being purchased, those rights must also be preserved. Any easements or other rights enjoyed under the
secure tenancy must be granted, and the property made subject to them, by the grant or conveyance.

For example, a landlord owns land through which
water and gas pipes pass. In owning the land, the landlord is
capable of granting access to these utilities. A secure tenant
on the land purchases her dwelling-house, which was supplied by those pipes during the secure tenancy. The landlord

therefore must grant access to these utilities (which become prescribed easements) in the grant or conveyance.

Further easements or rights can be added to the grant or conveyance, but the prescribed easements cannot be excluded or modified unless the tenant consents (HA 1985, Sched 6, para 2). The conveyance or grant must include provision for certain rights of way which are necessary for the reasonable enjoyment of the dwelling-house (HA 1985, Sched 6, para 3).

Restrictive covenants

Generally, a restrictive covenant is one which restricts the way the property may be used. The tenant must agree to be bound by certain restrictive covenants which affect the dwelling-house or to indemnify the landlord against breaches of those covenants. The most usual of these is that the property must not be used for business or other non-residential use.

Other covenants and conditions

The conveyance or grant may include "such covenants and conditions as are reasonable in the circumstances", but they are subject to other parts of Schedule 6 (see HA 1985, Sched 6, para 5). Any provision which purports to charge the lease-holder for the landlord's consent or approval is void (HA 1985, Sched 6, para 6).

Terms in the grant of a leasehold interest which are not the same as those in the secure tenancy agreement are not automatically unreasonable (see case number 93/B/1144, investigated by the Ombudsman and reported in *Inside Housing*, 29 July 1994).

Case report

Mr Guinan sought to exercise his right to buy the flat he rented from Enfield London Borough Council. The council offered him a lease on terms and conditions which were "standard" to all new leaseholders. This was done partly for administrative convenience. The tenant successfully applied in the county court for a declaration that certain terms in the lease were unreasonable. The council sought to argue that because leases on the same terms had been accepted by many other tenants the terms should not have been struck down. In the Court of Appeal Staughton LJ said that simply because the terms were in several thousand leases did not make unreasonable terms reasonable. It was open to the council to tell all the other tenants who had acquired the "standard" lease that it would not be insisting on the terms found to be unreasonable. A number of the challenges made by Mr Guinan were rejected; the court stressed that paragraph 5 of Schedule 6 does not permit the tenant to insist on positive covenants by the landlord (e.g. to employ a caretaker), but only to strike down those which were unreasonable. *Guinan v Enfield LBC* (1996) 29 HLR 456, CA.

The landlord may wish to include a covenant, for example, against harassment (see S Belgrave, *Nuisance and Harassment* (Arden's Housing Library) 1995, p 87, where a form of covenant is suggested). This becomes enforceable against subsequent purchasers of the property under section 33 of the Local Government (Miscellaneous Provisions) Act 1982.

Covenants to be included in freehold conveyances

Nature of interest

The conveyance shall be of an estate in fee simple absolute, subject only to limited burdens such as maintenance of structures for the benefit of the locality. The conveyance must be expressed to be made by the landlord as beneficial owner (HA 1985, Sched 6, Pt II).

Covenants to be included in grant of a lease

Where a lease is being granted, certain terms must be included (HA 1985, Sched 6, Pt III).

Nature of interest

The lease must be granted for the "appropriate term" and the ground rent must not exceed £10 per annum (HA 1985, Sched 6, para 11).

Rights to be included

For a flat where the tenant used common facilities, the lease must include the right to use those facilities, provided the landlord can grant that right. The right does not have to be included if the tenant agrees (HA 1985, Sched 6, para 13).

Covenants by landlord to repair and maintain

From a leaseholder's point of view the most important covenants by the landlord are those relating to the repair and maintenance of the property and, if it is a flat, of the block in which it is situated.

Where the dwelling-house is a flat, there are implied covenants by the landlord for repairs and maintenance (HA 1985, Sched 6, para 14(2)):

(a) the structure and exterior of the flat and the block in which it is situated (including drains, gutters and external pipes, and defects affecting the structure);

(b) any other property to which the tenant has rights (such as common facilities, rights of access, etc);

(c) services provided by the landlord to which the tenant is entitled (whether by him- or herself or in common with others) at a reasonable level and any installation connected with them.

It is also implied that the landlord shall rebuild or reinstate the dwelling-house in the event of damage by fire or flood etc or any other cause against which insurance is normally taken out (HA 1985, Sched 6, para 14(3)).

Where landlord is a leaseholder

Such covenants do not impose any obligation to repair and maintain where the landlord's lease, or any superior lease, provides otherwise (HA 1985, Sched 6, para 14(4)). If the obligations would have been imposed on the landlord had there not been a leasehold interest, the landlord by implied covenant must use its best endeavours to secure that the obligations under the superior lease are discharged. The landlord may be liable to contribute to the costs incurred by the superior landlord in carrying out these obligations, and the lease may require the tenant to bear a "reasonable part" of the contribution (see below).

There is a further implied covenant by the landlord "to pay the rent reserved by the landlord's lease and, except in so far as they fall to be discharged by the tenant, to discharge its obligations under the covenants contained in that lease". This covenant ensures that the landlord does not breach his own lease, thereby making that lease liable to forfeiture and thus possibly threatening the tenant's own lease.

Excluding the covenants

The only way implied covenants can be excluded or modified is by the parties' consent by way of application to the county. The court will not give its authorisation unless "it appears to the court that it is reasonable to do so" (HA 1985, Sched 6, para 14(4)). There is no provision to exclude or modify the covenant by the landlord to pay the rent and discharge the covenants in his own lease, by agreement or otherwise.

Covenants by tenant

Internal repairs

There is an implied covenant by the tenant:

> "(a) where the dwelling-house is a house, to keep the dwelling-house in good repair (including decorative repair);
> (b) where the dwelling-house is a flat, to keep the interior of the dwelling-house in such repair." (HA 1985, Sched 6, para 16).

The covenant may be excluded or modified by agreement between the parties, without a court order.

Service charges and other contributions

Schedule 6 includes a number of terms which must be included in the lease for the recovery of service charges. In addition to these statutory terms (which in general place limits on what landlords may claim) there is a large body of common law about the recovery of service charges which is outside the scope of this book; readers should consult D Kilcoyne *Leaseholds* (Arden's Housing Library) 1997. Any such provision in the lease which does not fall within the specific statutory regulations must comply with the general requirement that it is reasonable.

    The current statutory provisions were added to Schedule 6 by section 4(4) of the Housing and Planning Act 1986 with effect from 7 January 1987, inserted into Schedule 6 to HA 1985 as paras 16A – E.

Paragraph 16A allows a covenant requiring the tenant to bear "a reasonable part" of the landlord's costs incurred in discharging or insuring against repairs and maintenance. The landlord does not *have* to make any such provision, but if made it must be in accordance with paragraph 16A.

Normal insurance risks   In the case of normal insurance risks such as fire, the obligation is limited to a contribution to the cost of insurance and not the cost of discharge. (Even where there is no insurance, the tenant is liable to a reasonable sum in place of the contribution.) The tenant is entitled to inspect the insurance policy (at such reasonable times as may be specified in the lease) if he or she contributes to its cost (HA 1985, Sched 6, para 16A).

Superior landlords   Where the same obligations fall on the superior landlord rather than the landlord, the landlord may pass on some of the liability for its own service charges. The lease may require the tenant to bear a "reasonable part" of the landlord's contribution.

Improvements   The landlord may also wish to make improvements and to carry out other works outside the implied repair and maintenance obligations. Provision may be made in the lease for service charges to include the cost of such works but the covenant must be "reasonable in the circumstances" (HA 1985, Sched 6, para 5).

Limitations in the "initial period"   Generally, there is no restriction on when the period of liability for service charges begins, so the tenant can, provided it is reasonable to do so, be made liable for costs incurred before the grant. But liability for service charges and improvement contributions is restricted during an "initial period". Paragraph 16B deals with service charges in respect of repairs; paragraph 16C deals with improvement contributions; and paragraph 16E deals specifically with the right to acquire on rent to mortgage terms. Any provision in the lease which purports to authorise recovery outside the restrictions of those paragraphs is void (HA 1985, Sched 6, para 18). For service charges not affected by paragraphs 16B-16C, there is only a requirement that such provision be reasonable (HA 1985, Sched 6, para 5).

When the right to buy or to acquire on rent to mortgage terms is exercised the landlord must give information about service charges and improvement contributions in the section 125 notice. Under paragraphs 16B and 16C liability for service charges for repairs (including but not limited to the costs of meeting them) and improvement contributions is restricted during the first five years after the grant (or such other "initial period" as defined in paragraph 16B(4) (see below)). There is no restriction in the Housing Act 1985 on the amount of service charges which may be demanded after that period, but at common law service charges must be fair and reasonable (see further D Kilcoyne, *Leaseholder Management* (Arden's Housing Library) 1997).

Service charges for these purposes are defined in section 621A of the Housing Act 1985 as an "amount which is payable directly or indirectly for services, repairs, maintenance or insurance or the...lessor's costs of management and the whole or part of which varies according to the relevant costs". These restrictions accordingly do not apply to contributions to the cost of providing services other than the *variable* costs of repairs (including making good structural defects) and improvement contributions (e.g. the provision of caretaking services) (HA 1985, Sched 6, para 14(2)(c)).

Case report

Mr and Mrs Cole exercised their right to buy their flat from Coventry City Council. Under the terms of the lease they covenanted to pay a fixed service charge of £250 per annum. They refused to pay it and sought to argue that the charge could not be recovered during the initial period as it had not been included in the estimates. The Court of Appeal found that the charge was not limited under paragraph 16B. Furthermore the charge was reasonable under paragraph 5. *Coventry City Council v Cole* (1993) 25 HLR 555, CA.

The statutory definition of service charges includes charges for all services, so information about all service charges must be included in the section 125 notice. The tenant may have a claim for misrepresentation if there is a demand for certain service charges which is much greater than the estimated costs (see e.g. *Heinemann v Cooper* (1987) 19 HLR 262).

Itemised works of repair The tenant does not have to pay more than the amount shown in the section 125 notice as his or her estimated contribution, together with an inflation allowance, for itemised works of repair (HA 1985, Sched 6, para 16B(2)). The inflation allowance is calculated by a formula provided by paragraph 3 of the Housing (Right to Buy) (Service Charges) Order 1986.

Non-itemised works of repair For non-itemised works of repair, the tenant does not have to pay more than the "estimated annual average amount" of the service charge together with a different inflation allowance (HA 1985, Sched 6, para 16B(3)(a) and Housing (Right to Buy) (Service Charges) Order 1986, para 4). The estimated annual average in the section 125 notice will have been calculated over a period of about five years starting on the date the landlord hopes to have completed (section 125C). Where completion is delayed, this "reference period" may not be the same as the "initial period". So for any part of the initial period which continues after the reference period has come to an end, the average rate is used.

Improvement contributions   The tenant does not have to make any payment for improvements during the initial period where no estimate was given. If an estimate was given, the tenant does not have to pay more than the amount shown in the section 125 notice as his or her estimated contribution, together with an inflation allowance (HA 1985, Sched 6, para 16C).

The initial period   This is generally the five-year period starting with the date of the grant, but in some circumstances the "initial period" is different:

1. The lease may make provision for the payment of service charges or improvement contributions towards costs incurred in a period before the grant of the lease. In this case, the "initial period" of five years begins *before* the grant. The period starts with the beginning of the period of liability. However, few repairs carried out whilst the tenant is still a secure tenant are recoverable as service charges, because service charges may not be levied on repairs carried out in the discharge of the landlord's liability under section 11 of the Landlord and Tenant Act 1985 (see A Kilpatrick, *Repairs and Maintenance* (Arden's Housing Library) 1996).

2. The lease may make provision for service charges or improvement contributions to be calculated by reference to a specified annual period. The date of commencement of this period may not coincide with the date of grant. In this case, the "initial period" begins with the date of the grant and finishes with the end of the fifth specified annual period (although this may be after the fifth anniversary of the grant).

3. In cases where the (now repealed) right to defer completion has been exercised before 11 October 1993, the initial period begins before the grant of the lease. Time begins to run from date of deferral. The initial period ends on the date on which it would have ended if the lease had been granted on the date on which the section 142 (deferral) notice was served (Leasehold Reform, Housing and Urban Development Act 1993, s 137(2)).

Calculation of costs for those acquiring on rent to mortgage
Where the right to acquire on rent to mortgage terms is exercised (after 11 October 1993), the liability for costs incurred for repairs and improvement contributions before the final payment must not be more than the normal amount minus the landlord's percentage (HA 1985, Sched 6, para 16E).

Provisions affecting future disposals

Agreements in superior leases

Any provision in a lease held by the landlord or any superior landlord, or in any agreement, which purports to prohibit or restrict the grant of a lease to a secure tenant, whether by authorising a forfeiture or imposing a penalty or disability, is void. The same applies to a provision which purports to prohibit or restrict the subsequent disposal of a lease, for example by assignment or subletting (HA 1985, s 179; Sched 6, para 17 and 19).

Limitations on future disposals by tenants in National Parks

Tenants living in a National Park, an area of outstanding natural beauty, or area designated by the Secretary of State as a rural area, may exercise the right to buy in the same way as ordinary tenants. However, once they have purchased their property there may be restrictions on disposal. The property may only be sold to persons who work, or who have their only or principal home, in the area. The restriction does not apply to an exempted relevant disposal if it is through a compulsory disposal or disposal of land let with or used for the purposes of a dwelling-house. The grant of certain options is treated as a disposal (HA 1985, s 163).

Such limitations cannot be excluded from or modified in the lease agreement.

Case report

Mr and Mrs Milius lived in a flat above the newsagent they managed in Anglesey. They purchased the flat and shop below. A restriction on disposal, which had been approved by the Secretary of State, was designed to maintain an affordable supply of housing for local people. The provision prevented disposal without the local authority's consent, which could not be withheld if the disposal was to a person who throughout the preceding three years had had his place of work or his only or principal home within the Isle of Anglesey's rural areas. The applicants found they could not sell their property because no buyer could raise a mortgage, and so applied to the Lands Tribunal to be released from the restriction on the ground set out in section 84(1)(aa) of the Law of Property Act 1925 (i.e. that the continued existence of the covenant restricted the reasonable user of the land). The tribunal did not decide whether the restriction was a restrictive covenant such as would give them jurisdiction but, assuming that it did have the jurisdiction, found no ground for discharge. The tribunal heard evidence that the local authority had sold and was still selling properties subject to the restriction to purchasers who were assisted by mortgage lenders. Money would not be an adequate compensation for the authority and the restriction was not against the public interest. *Re Milius's Application* (1995) 70 P&CR 427.

7.
Loss and Enforcement of Right to Buy

Circumstances where right may be lost /
Change of tenant / Withdrawal and lapse
of right to buy / Enforcement and
resolution of disputes

In some circumstances tenants may lose the right to buy, or
the tenant may die or transfer the tenancy, in which case the
right may become unenforceable. This chapter looks first at
the circumstances where the right to buy may be lost,
secondly at the position where there is a change of tenant,
and thirdly at how the right may be enforced, if there is
entitlement to do so.

Circumstances where right may be lost

The right to buy is lost if the tenant loses security. This may
happen if there is a change in the landlord (see Chapter 8).
It may also happen if the tenant who has made the claim acts
in such a way that his or her status as a secure tenant is lost.

Loss of security

If the tenant ceases to be secure there is no entitlement to
the right to buy, since the right is dependent on a secure
tenancy (HA 1985, s 118). Security may be lost in several ways.

Only or principal home/subletting

The tenant must occupy the premises as his or her only or principal home for the tenancy to be secure. Similarly if the whole property is sublet it also ceases to be secure (HA 1985, s 93(2)).

Case reports

Mr and Mrs Jennings claimed the right to buy their flat, which was admitted by the council. Subsequently the tenants, who were elderly, moved out of the flat, which was then sublet, to rent a flat nearer their daughter. Mr Jennings then moved into a nursing home, and Mrs Jennings decided to stay in the rented accommodation to be near him. A date was proposed for completion on the right to buy, but the council then discovered that the flat had subsequently been sublet. The council refused to complete the sale, and sought possession of the flat. On appeal it was held that the tenants had ceased to be secure under section 93(2) of HA 1985 when they moved out. The right to buy was accordingly lost. *Jennings and Jennings v Epping Forest District Council* (1992) 25 HLR 241.

Mr and Mrs Thornley's right to buy was admitted by their housing association landlord, and a date set for completion. However, by this time the tenants had moved out to take up new employment, and sublet the house on an assured shorthold tenancy. The association discovered this in August 1990 and served notice to quit. The Court of Appeal held that the right was lost when the tenants vacated the premises. *Muir Group Housing Association v Thornley* (1992) 25 HLR 89.

Joint tenants

Where there is a joint tenancy, only one of the tenants need occupy the dwelling-house as his or her only or principal home. The tenant who ceases to occupy the dwelling-house does not thereby lose the right to buy.

The tenant's death

In some circumstances the tenant's death may lead to loss of the secure tenancy, although in others the right to buy may continue.

Continuation of the right   If there are joint tenants the survivor or survivors step into the shoes of the deceased tenant. If the stage has been reached so that the section 138 conditions are satisfied (i.e. all four procedural steps have been completed) the survivor can enforce the landlord's obligation to complete. If there are members of the deceased's family who qualify under section 123 and who have been required to share the right to buy under a valid section 123 notice, they must be treated as joint tenants and they too have the right of survivorship (*Harrow London Borough Council v Tonge* (1992) 25 HLR 99). This right applies even if the survivor is not a person qualified to succeed under section 87 of the HA 1985.

If no other person has been nominated, there may be a person qualified to succeed under section 87. The tenancy vests in them by virtue of section 89(2) of HA 1985 (see C Hunter, *Tenants' Rights* (Arden's Housing Library) 1995). That person can enforce the right to buy under section 136.

Loss of the right   If there is no nomination under section 123 and no person qualified to succeed, the right to buy is lost as the secure tenancy will have come to an end for these purposes (*City of Bradford Metropolitan Council v McMahon* (1993) 25 HLR 534).

Timing of loss of security

The tenant must be a secure tenant right up to the time the grant or conveyance comes to be made (see *London Borough of Sutton v Swann* (1985) 18 HLR 140 and *Muir Group Housing*

Association v Thornley (1992) 25 HLR 89). It is not sufficient for the tenant to be secure at the time of claiming the right to buy.

> **Case report**
>
> Mr Swann sought to exercise his right to buy from his landlord, the London Borough of Sutton. Stage 3 of the procedure had been reached, in that the Council had served its notice of offer but this had not yet been accepted by the tenant. The tenant moved out and bought a different property and ceased to be a secure tenant by the time the purchase came to be completed. It was held that he had lost the right to buy and could no longer accept the Council's terms. The basis for the decision was two-fold: that the offer had lapsed by effluxion of time and that "the status of secure tenant has to exist, not only at the time when the claim to buy is made, but also at the time when the grant comes to be made. If during the period between the claim and grant the tenant has ceased to be a secure tenant, he is not entitled to the grant". *London Borough of Sutton v Swann* (1985) 18 HLR 140.

Once step 4 in the procedure has been passed and the secure tenant has agreed terms, the landlord has a duty to complete and that duty may be enforced by injunction under section 138. Notwithstanding this right to an injunction at this stage the tenant may still lose the right to buy. The requirement that a tenant be secure continues up to the time of the grant. This is implicit in the relevant sections of the Act which refer to a "secure tenant" at every stage in the process, including section 155 which provides that a conveyance of the freehold shall contain "a covenant binding on the secure tenant". Tenants should be told that any change of circumstances must be notified to the landlord and a final check should be carried out prior to completion.

Delays by the landlord   In many cases there is a long period between agreeing terms and completion, often because of bureaucratic delays by the landlord. The question has arisen over whether, notwithstanding the loss of security, the tenant may proceed with the right to buy. The argument was put forward that the tenant acquired some form of "equitable" right to the property which was enforceable by the courts. This issue is most starkly illustrated by the following case.

> **Case report**
>
> Mrs McMahon was an elderly lady who had been living in her council house for about 40 years. In July 1990 she claimed the right to buy. In August 1990 her daughter and son-in-law moved to live with her. The Council admitted her right to buy and a notice of offer was served, which she accepted in November 1990. The Council was slow in making arrangements for the transfer and the tenant died in December 1991, before the conveyance had been executed. The daughter and son-in-law had not been nominated as sharers and did not qualify as successors within the meaning of section 87 of HA 1985 because they had not resided with the tenant for a sufficient period of time. The Council claimed possession against them. The Court of Appeal decided that the right to buy had been lost, even though there had been a long delay in executing the conveyance. Staughton LJ may have had some sympathy with the family when he suggested that the deceased tenant's estate may have a claim for damages for breach of statutory duty for failing to execute the conveyance. But it is notoriously difficult to obtain damages for breach of statutory duty unless there is clear statutory provision for doing so; there is no such provision HA 1985. *City of Bradford Metropolitan Council v McMahon* (1993) 25 HLR 534.

Discovering loss after completion

There is no reported case law which has examined the position of what can be done if it is not until after the completion of the exercise of the right to buy that the landlord discovers that the right has been lost at some stage in the proceedings.

A contract may in some circumstances be set aside on the grounds of mistake or misrepresentation.

Ineligibility for right to buy

There are two circumstances specifically referred to in HA 1985 in which the right to buy cannot be exercised (HA 1985, s 121):

> 1. where there is a court order requiring the tenant to give up possession; and
> 2. where there are certain bankruptcy proceedings.

The right to buy is not lost in these circumstances, but is put on hold. Therefore if the tenant ceases to fall within the bankruptcy provisions he or she may continue to exercise the right to buy. If the tenant goes back into possession after a temporary ouster injunction he or she may continue to exercise the right to buy, unless he or she has lost security. The tenant may have to re-serve his or her application or any other notices to exercise the right to buy, because in certain circumstances if there is considerable delay, the notice claiming to exercise the right to buy may be deemed to be withdrawn.

Order for possession

Under section 121(1), "The right to buy cannot be exercised if the tenant is obliged to give up possession of the dwelling-house in pursuance of an order of the court or will be so obliged at a date specified in the order". The section is not limited to possession orders made under the Act. A tenant may also be ordered to give up possession in matrimonial or domestic violence proceedings. Where a suspended possession order is obtained this is treated as an order for possession and thus disentitles the tenant from exercising

the right to buy. Tenants against whom an order for possession has been made, whether suspended or outright, may
seek to argue that if they are permitted to remain in possession, notwithstanding breach of the order, they have been
granted a new tenancy. In the light of the recent case law
(*Greenwich London Borough Council v Regan* (1996) 28 HLR
469, CA and *Burrows v Brent London Borough Council* (1996)
29 HLR 167, HL), it is quite unlikely that such an argument
will be successful, although each case must be considered on
its facts. Social landlords should be careful to ensure that
following a possession order they do not create new tenancies unless this is their explicit intention.

Joint tenants   A possession order is usually made against
both or all tenants under a joint tenancy, in which case none
of the tenants can exercise the right to buy.

In some circumstances an order may be made against
only one tenant, for example under the Matrimonial Homes
Act 1983 (soon to be replaced by the Family Law Act 1996).
Such an order is not usually sufficient to determine the joint
tenancy. Although the right to buy belongs automatically to
each tenant under a joint tenancy, the tenant who has left
under an order cannot exercise his or her right to buy. It
appears that the remaining tenant can complete under his or
her own right.

Timing of the order   Seeking a possession order against a tenant may take some time (see A Dymond, *Presenting
Possession Proceedings* (Arden's Housing Library) 1996).
Grounds for possession (e.g. arrears or nuisance behaviour)
may occur, but these need to be followed by a notice of seeking possession and a court hearing before the possession
order is sought. In the meantime, if the tenant proceeds with
the right to buy, provided the stage has not been reached
where the tenant can seek an injunction to force completion
under section 138, the right is lost.

Case report

Ms McKeon sought to exercise her right to buy. The stage had not yet been reached where section 138 came into operation. The right had been claimed and admitted by her landlord, the London Borough of Enfield, and the notice of offer had been served (stage 3 of the procedure), but the tenant had not yet agreed to the terms. In the meantime the landlord had served a notice of seeking possession on the basis of Ground 16 of Schedule 2 to HA 1985. Ms McKeon sought a declaration that she was entitled to complete the purchase of the property. The judge refused to grant the declaration and this was upheld in the Court of Appeal. The right to buy still needed to be "exercised". It was not too late for the Council to obtain an order for possession and thereby, under section 121, prevent the tenant from exercising the right to buy. *Enfield London Borough Council v McKeon* [1986] 1 WLR 1007, CA.

The position is rather different, though, where the tenant has reached a point where there is entitlement to complete the purchase. This is discussed further at p 104 below.

Insolvency Act proceedings

Under section 121(2) the right to buy cannot be exercised if the person, or one of the persons, to whom the right to buy belongs:

1. has a bankruptcy petition pending against him or her;

2. has a receiving order in force against him or her which was made before 29 December 1986;

3. is an undischarged bankrupt; or

4. has made a composition or arrangement with his or her creditors the terms of which remain to be fulfilled.

Once a tenant has been discharged, he or she may continue to exercise the right to buy.

Change of tenant

In some circumstances a secure tenancy may change hands. If the situation falls within section 136 of HA 1985 the landlord must then allow the new tenant to step into the old tenant's shoes. This means that the new tenant may take advantage of the discount offered to the old tenant (see *McIntyre v Merthyr Tydfil Borough Council* (1989) 21 HLR 320). The right must be transferred if:

1. there is a valid succession or assignment of the secure tenancy (except an assignment by way of exchange under section 92); or

2. the new tenant becomes the secure tenant under a periodic tenancy arising under section 86 on termination of a fixed-term secure tenancy (see HA 1985, s 136).

The transfer must be a genuine transfer rather than the creation of a new tenancy. Some landlords have a policy which purports to extend the statutory qualification for persons entitled to succeed to a tenancy; yet this will not be a succession but the grant of a new tenancy. Any attempt to assign a tenancy contrary to the section 91 provisions results in the creation of a new tenancy. If this is permitted by the landlord the new tenant has to make an application in his or her own right and may not be entitled to the same discount.

Where there has been a valid change of tenant under section 136 and a section 125 notice has already been served, the new tenant must serve a notice of intention (under section 125(D)) within 12 weeks. The time period starts when the tenant becomes a secure tenant or, if later, on service of the section 128(5) notice where there has been a valuation by the district valuer. The new tenant is required to serve a section 125(D) notice even if the old tenant had already served one. It is important that on a transfer of the tenancy the new tenant is made aware of the transfer of the right. The sanction for default on the part of the new tenant in serving the notice of intention is set out in section 125E.

The new tenant is not required to share the right to buy with members of the old tenant's family unless they are also members of his or her family (or would have been at the time the section 122 notice was served). Therefore members of the old tenant's family may lose the right to buy. Since the new tenant did not serve a section 122 notice, he or she cannot share the right with members of his or her family (HA 1985, s 136).

These provisions apply each time there is a new tenant.

Withdrawal and lapse of right to buy

Withdrawal and deemed withdrawal by tenant

The claim by the tenant may be withdrawn. The landlord does not have to take any further steps if the claim is withdrawn in writing (HA 1985, s 122(3)). In addition, inaction by the tenant may amount to withdrawal. The landlord's notice of admission lapses if no further action is taken by the tenant within a reasonable time (see *London Borough of Sutton v Swann* (1985) 18 HLR 140). In certain circumstances the statute penalises inactivity by a deemed withdrawal. Under section 125E if the tenant fails to give notice of intention to proceed and if a warning has been given, the notice of claim is deemed to be withdrawn. Also if the tenant fails to comply with a section 141 notice to complete, the claim is deemed to be withdrawn.

Withdrawal by landlord

Where there is entitlement to the right to buy the landlord cannot withdraw from the process. Where, however, the landlord makes a mistake or discovers a fact which means that the tenant was not entitled to the right to buy, it seems that the landlord may withdraw immediately. It was successfully argued in *James v Mansfield District Council* (28 October 1988, unreported, CA) that the steps leading up to completion are the establishment of a statutory right and are not based on a contract. The tenant either has the right or does not, so there is no breach of contract in refusing to complete the purchase to a tenant who does not have the right to buy.

Under section 177, where there is an error in the particulars required to be given in any notice by the tenant and the landlord mistakenly admits or denies the right to buy, or makes any decision based on a mistaken opinion as a result of the mistake, the tenant must be put in the position as if the mistake had not been made.

Enforcement and resolution of disputes

As already mentioned disputes over valuation must be referred to the district valuer. Other mechanisms for resolving disputes include application for an injunction, invoking the intervention of central government, or making an application for an order of mandamus in judicial review. Where maladministration is alleged, a complaint may also be made to the Ombudsman.

Injunctions and declarations

Intermediate stages

Where the landlord refuses or delays the completion of an intermediate stage, an injunction may be sought in the county court requiring compliance with the statutory duty. Where there is a dispute over entitlement (e.g. whether the tenant is secure) a declaration may be sought in the county court under section 181. A declaration can also be sought if the landlord fails to answer the tenant's claim at all. It has been suggested that the landlord has no duty to respond if the tenant is not in fact a secure tenant, because no valid claim has been made.

Enforcing completion

Once the tenant has claimed and established his or her right to buy and all matters relating to the grant have been agreed or determined, the landlord must convey the freehold or grant the lease under section 138(1) of HA 1985, so long as the tenant remains secure. The court is required to grant an injunction under section 138(3), if the section 138(1) conditions are satisfied (*Dance v Welwyn Hatfield District Council* [1990] 1 WLR 1097).

Conflict with possession actions   If the landlord obtains a possession order against the tenant prior to the stage where there is a right to completion, then the right to buy is lost. The possession process can be lengthy, and it may be the case that the tenant has established his or her right to buy prior to the landlord making much progress with the possession action. Whether the tenant is entitled to an injunction enforcing completion where the landlord intends to or is seeking possession has been considered in a number of cases. They concluded that the completion cannot be delayed while the landlord seeks possession. The court has no discretion and cannot consider matters such as hardship to third parties.

Case report

Mrs Taylor and her landlord, the London Borough of Newham, had agreed all outstanding matters relating to the right to buy of her house. Before completion the landlord became aware of allegations that the tenant and her family were causing a nuisance to neighbours and committing acts of racial harassment. The landlord commenced possession proceedings and argued that the court had discretion to refuse an injunction to complete under section 138(3). It was held that the grant of the injunction was mandatory once the conditions were satisfied. They were satisfied in this case. The court may however refuse an injunction on the grounds of mistake, misrepresentation, or fraud, because these are grounds for saying that the conditions in section 138(1) had not been fulfilled. None of those grounds were made out in the case, and the court held that the injunction could not be refused simply on the basis of general hardship, in this case to other tenants. *Taylor v Newham London Borough Council* [1993] 1 WLR 444, CA.

Even in an extreme case, where there is very strong evidence that a tenant is in breach of the tenancy conditions, the landlord must act quickly in bringing possession proceedings.

Case report

Mr Lovell sought to exercise his right to buy, and his landlord, Bristol City Council, served a section 125 notice setting out the terms on 30 June 1994. On 4 July 1994 the landlord issued a notice of seeking possession on the basis that the property was being used by Mr Lovell as a centre for drug dealing. Proceedings for possession were issued on 21 September 1994. On 14 October Mr Lovell accepted the terms of the right to buy offer. The defendant denied the allegations made by the landlord, and counterclaimed in its possession proceedings for an injunction enforcing his right to buy. The judge granted the injunction, and held that accordingly the possession proceedings did not require to be resolved. The Court of Appeal, somewhat reluctantly but in the light of the decisions in earlier cases, upheld the injunction granted in the county court. As the possession order had not actually been obtained, there could be no reason for not granting the injunction under section 136(1). *Bristol City Council v Lovell* (1996) 29 HLR.

Judicial review

In most cases decisions made are relatively straightforward: there is no room to exercise discretion, and most procedural requirements are mandatory. But there may be disputes which are much less clear cut, for example about whether a tenant was a public sector tenant during the qualification period. The court may entertain an application for judicial review if a landlord (who is a public body, though this does not include housing associations) acts unreasonably or in breach of the rules of natural justice. An application is unlikely to succeed unless all other remedies have been exhausted. Therefore, where it is open to the tenant to make an application for a declaration in the county court to resolve a dispute, he or she may be encouraged to do so. The Secretary of State's default powers under section 164 (and following sections) may be taken into account as an alternative avenue of redress, but this is not a right of appeal and it is likely that the court would entertain an application for judicial review if the landlord was acting unreasonably.

Jurisdiction was accepted under Order 53 of the Rules of the Supreme Court (i.e. for judicial review) in *R v Council of the City of Plymouth and Cornwall County Council, ex p John Charles Freeman* ((1986) 18 HLR 243) where among other matters the question of whether an authority's decision that the landlord condition was not satisfied was in issue.

> ### Example
>
> An applicant may, for example, claim to be living with his or her spouse at the time an application is made (so that a period during which the spouse was a public sector tenant may be taken into account). If the authority decides not to believe the tenant there must be a factual basis for its decision. So if the spouse in interview claims that he or she separated from the tenant many years ago and is a tenant of the authority in another property, the authority may be entitled to disbelieve the tenant's claim. It would

usually be unfair not to give the tenant the opportunity to explain him- or herself or answer the allegation that he or she is not telling the truth. The tenant's remedy in this case is to seek a declaration in the county court that he or she qualified for the period claimed. The tenant may also make an application for judicial review on the ground of breach of natural justice.

Intervention of Secretary of State

Direct intervention

If the landlord does not deal with claims "effectively and expeditiously", the tenant may try to invoke the Secretary of State's powers to intervene under section 164. The Secretary of State has wide-ranging powers to intervene by taking any action which appears to him or her "necessary or expedient" to enable secure tenants to exercise the right to buy. For example, a tenant may complain about the speed with which his or her claim is being processed, or about a policy which the landlord has in dealing with claims.

Before the Secretary of State decides to intervene, he or she can obtain information from the landlord under section 169 to assist in making the decision.

Once the decision to intervene has been made, but before any powers are exercised, the Secretary of State must serve notice on the landlord under section 164(2). The Secretary of State may exercise his or her powers while the notice is in force and before it is withdrawn under section 166. The notice is deemed to be given 72 hours after it has been sent, so the landlord usually has a few days before any action is taken to make objections or to take any steps to remedy the complaint.

Once the notice takes effect the Secretary of State takes over the whole process. The landlord may not take any steps other than those permitted or required by the notice. If the landlord does take any step which is not permitted by the notice, the action has no effect.

The Secretary of State has the general power to carry out the sale or rent to mortgage using whatever steps are necessary. He or she is not limited to following all the steps the landlord must follow, (i.e. he or she is not bound to follow the procedure provided the sale or acquisition is valid under the Act).

The Secretary of State may enter into correspondence with the landlord, and hold meetings and inquiries. He or she has a free reign in the conduct of any inquiry.

Case report

The Secretary of State intervened in a case in which tenants complained that Norwich City Council was taking too long to make initial price valuations. Letters were exchanged and the Secretary of State had meetings with the councillors and officers of the Council. It appeared that valuations would be conducted more speedily if they were dealt with in the first instance by the district valuer. The Council did not wish to use the district valuer because of his quasi judicial capacity. The then Secretary of State and the Minister of State for Housing took part personally in the meetings. The councillors and officers were warned of the personal consequences they faced (e.g. their default might amount to "wilful misconduct" with liability to make good any loss and the possibility of disqualification from acting as councillors). The council made a formal reply, and then the Secretary of State made his formal decision (i.e. he gave notice of intention to intervene), concluding that the council's conduct could well amount to non-compliance with the statutory requirements and that the "tenants have or may have difficulty in exercising the right to buy effectively and expeditiously". The Council was unsuccessful in its application to the High Court and on appeal for an order of certiorari to quash the decision to intervene and for an injunction to stop him acting upon his notice. *R v Secretary of State for the Environment, ex p Norwich City Council* [1982] QB 808, CA.

As well as his or her general powers of intervention, the Secretary of State is given various specific powers to ensure that the intervention is successful in achieving enforcement of the right to buy procedure. Under section 165, he or she has the specific power to make a vesting order which has the effect of a conveyance or grant. Thus, although not the owner of the land, the Secretary of State can effectively convey it. If the landlord suffers any loss as a result of a registration made on production of the vesting order, and would otherwise be entitled to be indemnified by the Chief Land Registrar, the Secretary of State must indemnify the landlord instead.

The Secretary of State has the specific power to give directions on covenants and conditions to be included in the conveyance under section 167. The Secretary of State can thus prevent terms being included if it appears to him or her that the grant or conveyance would not conform with the Act. For example under paragraph 5 of Schedule 6 the landlord may include "such covenants and conditions as are reasonable in the circumstances". A dispute over whether a term is reasonable may be resolved by the county court under section 181 or by the Secretary of State. Where the offending term is already included in the grant or conveyance, the Secretary of State has the power to discharge or modify it under section 168. If this is done, the landlord must notify the owner of the property, any owner of a charge on it, and the Chief Land Registrar (who will not require the land certificate) that the change has been made (HA 1985, s 168). The Secretary of State may also by notice in writing require the landlord to supply information or produce any document (HA 1985, s 169).

The Secretary of State's intervention comes to an end with the service of a section 166 notice. The landlord resumes conduct of the proceedings subject to any direction which is contained in that notice. An account is drawn up. Any money held or received by the Secretary of State on behalf of the landlord must be passed on, without interest. This may be set off against the costs of intervention, together with interest, which must be paid by the landlord upon receipt of a certificate from the Secretary of State.

If the landlord is unhappy with the intervention or denies that the tenants have or may have difficulty in exercising the right to buy effectively and expeditiously, it should first ask the Secretary of State to withdraw the notice. If the Secretary of State refuses, the landlord may apply to the High Court for judicial review of the Secretary of State's decision to intervene. The Secretary of State may intervene if "it appears to him" that a tenant or tenants "have or may have difficulty" exercising effectively and expeditiously the right to buy. It was held in *R v Secretary of State for the Environment, ex p Norwich City Council* [1982] QB 808, CA that the Secretary of State does not have to show that the landlord has acted unreasonably or is in breach of any statutory duty before he or she intervenes. It is enough if there are facts on which he or she could reasonably conclude that tenants might have difficulty. Any final decision of the Secretary of State is open to judicial review.

Financial assistance

The Secretary of State may provide financial assistance under section 170. If there is a dispute between the tenant or his or her successor and the landlord (other than a dispute about valuation) which gives rise to litigation the Secretary of State may grant a form of "legal aid" in certain circumstances to allow the tenant to pursue the action. Financial assistance is available where the case raises a question of principle, or it is unreasonable to expect the applicant for assistance to deal with the case without this special class of assistance, having regard to the complexity of the case or to any other matter, or on account of any other special consideration. The type of assistance is similar to that provided by ordinary legal aid but may include giving advice, negotiating a settlement, and arranging for legal representation (including representation by the Treasury Solicitor). There is no means test. The assistance forms the basis for a first charge on any costs recovered, subject to any charge in favour of the Legal Aid Board (e.g. where the tenant has been legally aided before (or after) the Secretary of State's intervention).

8.
Changes in the Landlord's Interest

Right to buy was (or was about to be) admitted before landlord's disposal of property / Right to buy already (or about to be) denied / Completion already taken place / Preservation of right to buy

The landlord may change during the right to buy process; for example a local authority landlord may transfer its stock to a housing association. Where this occurs the tenants may lose the right to buy if they cease to be secure tenants and become assured tenants. In some circumstances, such as a stock transfer between authorities, the tenant remains secure and entitled to exercise the right to buy. The statutory provisions seek to protect the right to buy in these circumstances, but the position varies depending on the stage the procedure has reached.

Right to buy was (or was about to be) admitted before landlord's disposal of property

Landlord condition satisfied

If the new landlord satisfies the "landlord condition" and none of the Schedule 5 exceptions applies the tenant continues to exercise the right to buy and the new landlord automatically steps into the old landlord's shoes. The new landlord is deemed to be in the same position as the old one without further notices having to be served (HA 1985, s 137(1)). This is not the case where the type of interest owned by the new landlord differs in any "material respect" (e.g. is a leaseholder rather than a freeholder) from that owned by the old landlord. In this event further steps may need to be taken (e.g. notices amended or reserved, time extended, etc) to put the tenant as nearly as may be in the same position as if the transfer had taken place before the claim (HA 1985, s 137(2)). The new landlord is likely to have to re-serve all the notices that were already served by the old landlord.

If the new landlord satisfies the section 30 landlord condition but one of the Schedule 5 exceptions now applies, the right to buy is lost. Any notices which have been served on the tenant must be withdrawn.

Landlord condition not satisfied

If the new landlord does not meet the section 30 landlord condition the right to buy is normally lost, but there are some circumstances where it is preserved under section 171A. Even if the right is so preserved, it may still be lost if one of the Schedule 5 exceptions applies. Where the right to buy is preserved, the new landlord steps into the old landlord's shoes, as above, unless the new interest is different (HA 1985, s 171H).

Right to buy already (or about to be) denied

Landlord condition satisfied

Where the right to buy has been denied, the new landlord must review the situation. If one of the Schedule 5 exceptions applies to the new landlord, no further steps need be taken, as the right has already been denied. If the new landlord satisfies the section 80 landlord condition and none of the exceptions applies, the right must be admitted.

Where the right must now be admitted, and the old landlord had already served a section 124 notice denying the right, that notice must be withdrawn and re-served as soon as practicable. If any time period needs to be extended to allow the tenant to exercise any rights, the extension must be given. Essentially all parties must take whatever steps are necessary to put the tenant in the same position as he or she would have been if the transfer had taken place before the tenant's notice of claim was served (HA 1985, s 137(2)).

Landlord condition not satisfied

If the new landlord does not satisfy the section 80 landlord condition the right is normally denied, but there are cases where it is preserved (see below) (HA 1985, s 171A).

Completion already taken place

There is a requirement in section 154 of HA 1985 that title must be registered. If a lease is not registered, any new landlord may take free of the lease, because it is not an overriding interest. The tenant has a claim against the former landlord for failing to register the lease.

In any event, if registration is not applied for within two months of the conveyance or grant, the legal title to the leasehold or freehold reverts to the landlord, although the law may impose some sort of trust.

Preservation of right to buy

Where there is a transfer to a landlord who does not satisfy the landlord condition, so that the tenant is no longer a secure tenant, the tenant may nonetheless be entitled to the preserved right to buy.

Qualification for preserved right

The preserved right to buy arises where a secure landlord disposes of a dwelling-house to a non-secure landlord, thereby causing the tenancy to cease to be secure (HA 1985, s 171A).

Exceptions to preserved right

The right to buy cannot be preserved where one of the exceptions stated in paragraphs 1-3 of Schedule 5 applied to the *former* landlord. Those exceptions are charities, co-operative housing associations, and housing associations which at no time received certain public grants. The Secretary of State can make other exceptions.

Qualifying persons

Those who enjoy the preserved right are listed in section 171B(2). These "qualifying persons" include:

1. the former secure tenant or each joint tenant;
2. a person who becomes the joint tenant of a person who has the preserved right to buy;
3. where a former secure tenant having the preserved right to buy died or assigned his tenancy, a member of his or her family who took his or her place;
4. a person who becomes the tenant under a property adjustment order or transfer on divorce or separation under section 1 of the Matrimonial Homes Act 1983 (or, when it comes into force, the Family Law Act 1996).

The preserved rights

The qualifying person in essence retains the right to buy the property, but subject to modifications. The modifications are made by the relevant regulations. The Housing (Preservation of the Right to Buy) Regulations 1993 (SI No 2241) is the most recent legislation at the time of writing, and affects all claims made on or after 11 October 1993. The Regulations set out in Schedule 2 all the parts of HA 1985 which have been amended. Once it has been established that the preserved right to buy applies, immediate reference may be made to the Regulations rather than to HA 1985.

Modifications to reflect "qualifying persons"

Because the term "qualifying person" is used in respect of the preserved right to buy, the more restrictive term "tenant" as used in the Housing Act must be substituted by the term "qualifying person" in certain sections. Also, because the tenant may move to another dwelling-house owned by the same landlord (or connected company), the term "dwelling-house" must in some sections be substituted by the term "qualifying dwelling-house".

Main modifications

The main modifications to HA 1985 are as follows:

1. There is no right to acquire on rent to mortgage terms (HA 1985, s 143). Reference to that right is omitted where it arises in the Act.

2. The new landlord has absolute discretion over whether to include a covenant to repay the discount in the conveyance or grant (HA 1985, s 155). If the landlord does chose to insert such a covenant, it must not be more onerous than the one prescribed by section 155.

3. If the new landlord is a local authority or the

Development Board for Rural Wales, the provisions for the restriction of disposal of dwelling-houses in National Parks etc do not apply. For other landlords, certain restrictions are removed (HA 1985, s 157).

4. The Secretary of State does not have the power to intervene (HA 1985, ss 164-70).

5. There is no power to extend the right to buy.

6. It appears that there is no requirement for prescribed forms to be used (HA 1985, s 176).

7. There are different provisions for limiting the amount of discount which may be made. A new Schedule 5A is inserted into the Act. It deals with relevant costs and ascertainment of the cost floor.

8. The new landlord does not have the power to match the term of the lease which is granted on a flat to the terms of other flats in the building (HA 1985, Sched 6, para 12(3)).

In addition, when the new landlord executes the conveyance or lease to the qualifying person, there must be a term in the conveyance or grant stating whether the transfer was in pursuance of the preserved right to buy (HA 1985, Sched 9A, para 7(1), (2)).

Moves by the tenant

If the qualifying person moves, the preserved right to buy may in some cases be retained. Usually the qualifying person must continue to occupy the dwelling-house as his or her only or principal home, and accordingly if he or she moves out the right is lost. However, if the move is to another dwelling-house owned by the same landlord or a connected company, whether voluntarily or under a court order (e.g. under HA 1988, Sched 2, ground 9, on the provision of suitable alternative accommodation) the preserved right continues and moves with the qualifying person (HA 1985, s 171B(6)). If possession is sought against someone with the preserved right then the landlord is prevented from obtaining the order unless the court is satisfied that the right to buy is preserved and that the landlord has at least the same type of interest in the new dwelling-house (HA 1985, s 171F). There are no such restrictions if, as a result of the move, the landlord satisfies the section 80 landlord condition, since at that point the tenant becomes entitled to the full right to buy.

Disposal of landlord's interest

At the time of the initial disposal by the original landlord, certain provisions must be complied with to protect the qualifying person.

When the transfer is made to the new landlord under the preserved right to buy, there are various terms which must be included in any conveyance or grant executed under that right (see HA 1985, s 171G and Sched 9A for such terms and registration requirements). The conveyance or grant must include notice stating that the right to buy was preserved and describing the dwelling-house. The conveyance or grant must be registered, if it is not already registered, in the same way that the conveyance or grant to a tenant exercising the right to buy must be registered. The Chief Land Registrar's certificate must be given to the new landlord.

Provided the paragraph 1 statement is included in the lease or grant, the Chief Land Registrar enters the preserved right to buy as a notice and restriction on the register at the same time as title is registered. If the landlord fails to include the notice so that the preserved right to buy is not registered and as a result is lost, it becomes liable to compensate the qualified person or indemnify the Chief Land Registrar. In respect of registered title, no certificate is necessary unless the Chief Land Registrar asks for it from the landlord. If the right is not registered, it may be lost. If the landlord fails to register the right the qualifying person may do so.

Further disposals of landlord's interest

Where there is a second change in the landlord's interest, the preserved right to buy is generally not affected, except in two cases (HA 1985, s 171D).

Landlord condition satisfied by new landlord

Where the new landlord satisfies the section 30 landlord condition and none of the Schedule 5 exceptions applies, the tenant continues to exercise the right to buy. It is no longer the preserved right to buy. There must be a statement in the conveyance or grant to the effect that the preserved right to buy has come to an end and that the right to buy is being exercised. The next landlord steps into the shoes of the previous one (see above) unless its interest is materially different (HA 1985, Sched 9A, para 7(3); s 171H).

Unregistered preserved right

Under Schedule 9A, if the preserved right to buy was not registered the next landlord may acquire the interest free of that right. The right is not an overriding interest, and accordingly failure to register the rights means that they will be lost on a subsequent disposal (unless of course the landlord satisfies the section 30 condition above, in which case there is no need to preserve the right). Where the landlord fails to comply with the duty to register the preserved right, the tenant is entitled to compensation (HA 1985, Sched 9A, para 6).

Disposal of part of landlord's interest

There is an absolute prohibition under section 171D(2) on disposal by a landlord of part of its interest (and this may include the grant of a lease) unless:

1. it has the Secretary of State's consent; or

2. the disposal is to the qualifying person or persons (disposal to only one of several qualifying persons is unlikely to exempt the landlord from requiring consent); or

3. there was failure to register the right (see above) and the next landlord took the interest free of the right.

Termination of landlord's interest

If the landlord's interest is terminated (e.g. by forfeiture, surrender, or expiry of a lease) the right ceases to be pre-served (HA 1985, s 171E). If the landlord applies for relief from forfeiture, the right to buy probably remains preserved. It is open to the tenant to apply for relief him- or herself. In this case the lease is transferred to the tenant without involv-ing the right to buy procedure.

If the termination is the landlord's fault, the qualifying person can seek compensation from the landlord for the loss of the preserved right to buy. Compensation is payable if the termination was due to any "act or omission" of the land-lord. It is not necessary to prove negligence. The landlord is liable for the loss of the discount and probably for non-monetary loss from the date of loss.

Extended right to buy

The tenant may have the right to buy the freehold from a superior landlord (see Chapter 9). That right cannot be preserved.

9.
Extension of Right

Legislation / When does extended right
apply? / Modifications of right to buy /
Procedure / Right to acquire on rent to
mortgage terms / Tenant's notice of delay /
Registration of title / Repayment of
discount / Secretary of State's power to
intervene / Assistance to freeholder /
Inclusion of land / Covenants in the
conveyance

If the secure tenant's immediate landlord is a leaseholder, the
tenant may be able to buy out that landlord and buy the freehold of (or acquire on rent to mortgage terms) his house
directly from the freeholder. This is known as the extended
right to buy.

Legislation

Under section 171 of HA 1985 the Secretary of State can, by
order, extend the right to buy or acquire on rent to mortgage
terms. The current regulations at the time of writing are the
Housing (Extension of Right to Buy) Order 1993 (SI No
2240). If there is any doubt about whether any part of the
right to buy pro-visions in HA 1985 have been modified,
reference must be made both to the Act and to the
Regulations. Unfortunately there is no alternative to this
unwieldy process, unlike the case of the preserved right to

buy where the amended Act is set out in full in the Regulations.

When does extended right apply?

The right to buy is extended if the dwelling-house is a "house" and if the freehold, and any intermediate interest including the immediate landlord's interest, is held by one of the following authorities or bodies:

- a local authority
- a new town corporation
- a housing action trust
- an urban development corporation
- the Development Board for Rural Wales
- the Housing Corporation or Housing for Wales
- a registered housing association, other than one excepted from the right to buy by Schedule 5, paragraphs 1 (charities), 2 (co-operatives) and 3 (associations which have not received a grant).

Modifications of right to buy

In these circumstances, the legislative provisions for claiming the right to buy or to acquire on rent to mortgage terms are modified. Most of the modifications concern the service of notices and ensure that all parties in the chain of interests are informed about what is happening to the tenant's claim. Because the landlord is not the freeholder, certain references to "the landlord" in the Act are substituted by "freeholder" or "landlord or intermediate landlord or freeholder". The freeholder and intermediate landlords are brought within the ambit of various provisions in the Act which only apply to the immediate landlord.

Other references to and connected with leases or flats are omitted. Major changes are explained in outline below but reference should be made to the relevant regulations for full details of the modifications.

Procedure

Claiming the right to buy

A new section 122A is inserted in the Act so that where the right has been claimed, the notice must be passed on up the chain to the freeholder. Each landlord has a duty to pass the notice on to his immediate landlord. When a section 122 notice is served by the tenant, the landlord must, as soon as practicable, serve a copy on the superior landlord and serve on the tenant a notice in writing that this has been done. The notice must be passed on in this way until it reaches the freeholder. If at any stage any landlord knows of any reasons for denying the right, this must be stated when the notice is served.

Admitting or denying the right

Section 124 is modified so that the freeholder has eight weeks to serve copies of the section 124 notice on everyone. If at any time the interest of any party in the chain of interests passes to an authority or body not on the list above, it is the freeholder's duty to inform the tenant that he or she is no longer entitled to buy or acquire the freehold. The tenant may still be able to buy or acquire the leasehold from the immediate landlord.

Withdrawal of tenant's notice

Section 122(3) is omitted and replaced with a new section 124A. If the tenant wishes to withdraw before he or she has received the freeholder's section 124 notice he or she may do so by notice in writing to the immediate landlord. When the immediate landlord receives such a notice it must be passed on up the chain to the freeholder. If the tenant wishes to withdraw after receiving the freeholder's section 124 notice, he or she must serve the notice of withdrawal on the freeholder, who must pass it back down the chain.

Notice of offer

References to improvement contributions in the various sections is omitted. Section 125 is modified so that after the right has been established, the freeholder has 12 weeks to serve on the tenant the notice of terms. Section 125A(3) is omitted so that the freeholder does not have to give estimates for work that may be incurred.

Change of landlord or tenant

Where there is a change of secure tenant after claiming the right to buy, section 136 is modified so that a notice of change must be passed up the chain. Section 137 is also modified so that if there is a change in the interest (or if any interest comes to an end) of any landlord in the chain (including the freeholder), that landlord must notify the tenant direct. The landlord must also notify the next landlord in the chain, who must in turn pass on the notification. The new interest holder steps into the shoes of the old one.

A change of landlord or intermediate landlord or freeholder does not affect the extended right to buy so long as the new landlord is on the list of landlords who qualify under the Housing (Extension of Right to Buy) Order. The extended right is lost if the new landlord, including any landlord in the chain and the freeholder, is not on the list. It is the freeholder's duty, in these circumstances, to notify the tenant in writing that he or she is no longer entitled to acquire the freehold. The tenant may still be able to buy the leasehold from his or her immediate landlord by exercising his or her right to buy in the usual way. The question of whether the extended right to buy is lost is a simple one. There is no equivalent of the preserved right to buy.

Apportionment of purchase price

The full purchase price is paid by the tenant to the free-holder. There are special provisions on completion for part of the purchase price to be passed on by the freeholder to the landlord and any intermediate landlord (or owner of a rent charge) for loss of the lease (HA 1985, s 138A). There is no duty to compensate for a lease if the residue of the term is less than a year immediately before completion or if the lease is for a periodic tenancy. The amount that the freeholder must pay to the landlord, each intermediate landlord and any owner of a rent charge on any lease in the chain is determined by a formula set out in section 138A.

There is a requirement that any landlord must assist the freeholder in providing information to calculate the formula. This is in addition to the provisions which require any landlord to give general assistance to the freeholder (HA 1985, s 177A.

Execution of conveyance

Section 139(1A) is inserted. The freeholder must execute the conveyance on its own behalf and in the names of any landlords. The conveyance is binding on all the authorities or bodies named. There must be a statement in the conveyance that section 139(1A) applies. Section 139(2) is modified so that not only does the secure tenancy come to an end, but also the lease of the landlord and any superior landlord.

Right to acquire on rent to mortgage terms

The 1993 Regulations take into account this right which was introduced with effect from 11 October 1993.

Claiming the right

On receipt of the tenant's section 144 notice claiming the right, it is the landlord's duty to pass the notice to the free-holder directly and to any intermediate landlords. This is unlike the section 122 claim to the right to buy, where each landlord's duty is limited to passing the notice to the superior landlord and so on up the chain. The landlord must state to each authority or body when serving the notice:

    1. whether to its knowledge the tenant is precluded from exercising the right, and

    2. the current amount of the weekly rent.

Admitting or denying the right

Section 146 provisions are only altered in so far as references to the landlord are replaced by references to the freeholder. Accordingly, the notice admitting or denying the right does not have to be passed to the landlord or any intermediate landlord.

Withdrawal of notice

Section 144(4) is omitted and replaced with section 144A. The provisions are similar to those which extend the right to buy. If the tenant wishes to withdraw before he or she has received the freeholder's section 146 notice he or she may do so by notice in writing to the immediate landlord. When the immediate landlord receives such a notice the landlord must pass the notice to the freeholder directly and to any inter-mediate landlords (rather than the notice being passed up the chain by each landlord in turn). If the tenant wishes to withdraw after receiving the freeholder's section 146 notice, he or she must serve the notice of withdrawal on the freeholder, who must pass it to each landlord in the chain directly. There is nothing to stop the tenant exercising the right to buy after he or she has withdrawn the claim to acquire on rent to mortgage terms.

Change of landlord

These provisions under section 149, as modified, are the same as the provisions extending the right to buy under section 136. Where there is disposal to a private sector landlord there is no preserved right to buy.

Apportionment of initial payment

The initial payment is paid by the tenant to the freeholder. A new section 150A is inserted by the 1993 Regulations so that on completion, the freeholder must pay to the landlord and any intermediate landlord (or owner of a rent charge) for loss of the lease. There is no duty to compensate for a lease if the residue of the term is less than a year immediately before completion or if the lease is for a periodic tenancy. The amount that the freeholder must pay to the landlord, each intermediate landlord and any owner of a rent charge on any lease in the chain is determined by a formula set out in the section.

There is also a new provision under section 150B which gives the parties the power to agree to whatever apportionment they consider fair and reasonable.

Execution of conveyance

There are similar provisions to those which extend the right to buy. Section 151(1A) is inserted. The freeholder must execute the conveyance on its own behalf and in the names of any landlords. The conveyance is binding on all the authorities or bodies named. There must be a statement in the conveyance that section 151(1A) applies. Section 151(2) is modified so that not only the secure tenancy comes to an end, but also the lease of the landlord and any superior landlord.

Redemption of freeholder's share

The obligation, when certain disposals are made, to make a final payment to redeem the landlord's share must be contained in a covenant in the conveyance (see HA 1985, Sched 6A). The share is paid directly to the freeholder. It must then be apportioned amongst the landlords in accordance with paragraph 7A of Schedule 6A. There is no duty to compensate for a lease if the residue of the term is less than a year immediately before completion or if the lease is for a periodic tenancy. The amount that the freeholder must pay to the landlord, each intermediate landlord and any owner of a rent charge on any lease in the chain is determined in accordance with a formula set out in the section.

Tenant's notice of delay

The 1993 Regulations modify the provisions for this procedure in sections 153A and 153B (which came into operation on 10 March 1989) so that the notices are served on and by the authority or body which is responsible for the delay.

Registration of title

A new subsection (5A) is added to section 154 so that where the lease of the landlord or any intermediate landlord is registered, the freeholder must use its best endeavours to obtain and produce to the Chief Land Registrar that lease and its appropriate land or charge certificate.

Repayment of discount

Any discount repayable is paid by the tenant to the freeholder on disposal. There are provisions for apportioning the discount recovered amongst the various landlords in the chain (HA 1985, s 156A). There is no duty to pay any landlord in the chain if the residue of the term is less than a year immediately before completion or if the lease is for a periodic tenancy. The amount that the freeholder must pay to the landlord, each intermediate landlord and any owner of a rent charge on any lease in the chain is determined by a formula set out in the section.

If the right to acquire on rent to mortgage terms has been exercised, this apportionment is subject to the section 150 power to agree final apportionment.

Secretary of State's power to intervene

New provisions are inserted under section 164(5A) which allow the Secretary of State to take action against any intermediate landlord or the freeholder. By section 166A the section 164 and 166 notices must be served on all the other parties in the chain.

Assistance to freeholder

The landlord and any intermediate landlord must, on written request, provide the freeholder with any information and assistance it requires to process the tenant's claim. Such landlords must also ensure that all deeds and other documents are available to the tenant on conveyance of the property to him or her; these include, where the land is registered, the land certificate and other necessary documents required by the tenant to perfect his or her title to the property, where that title is not to be registered.

Inclusion of land

Where land is included in the tenant's claim as a part of the dwelling-house, notices relating to it must be served on all the parties in the chain (HA 1985, s 184, as amended, and further subsections added by the 1993 Regulations). Reference should be made to the 1993 Regulations for details of service.

Covenants in the conveyance

Various modifications are made to Schedule 6. A new paragraph 4A on indemnities states:

> "Where the freeholder is aware of an obligation relating to the dwelling-house breach of which may expose the landlord or an intermediate landlord to liability to another person, the freeholder shall include in the conveyance such provision (if any) as may be reasonable in the circumstances to relieve the landlord or intermediate landlord (as the case may be) from, or to indemnify him against, that liability."

There is a new paragraph 21A on charges. Where a lease is extinguished when the freehold is purchased, any charge on that lease remains as a personal obligation of the landlord or intermediate landlord. (Also see Chapter 6 above).

10.

Housing Associations and Other Registered Social Landlords

Housing associations within the right to buy /
Housing associations outside the right to buy /
Tenants' incentive scheme / Right to acquire
under Housing Act 1996 / Voluntary sales

Although primarily it is the stock of local authority dwellings which has been affected by the right to buy, secure tenants of some housing associations also enjoy the right to buy. However, since 15 January 1989 (the date on which the Housing Act 1988 came into force) all new housing association tenants have been assured, and are thus outside the right to buy. This means that the rights of such tenants were considerably less than those whose tenancies had been granted before this date. While the voluntary Tenants' Incentive Scheme did enable some tenants to buy their own home, it was not until the introduction of the right to acquire under the Housing Act 1996 that commensurate rights were given to assured tenants. The 1996 Act also introduced the new concept of registered social landlords, and it is the tenants of these landlords who have been given the right to acquire.

Housing associations within the right to buy

Until 15 January 1989 housing association tenants were secure tenants and accordingly had the right to buy their property unless the landlord fell within any of the exceptions in Schedule 5. Such tenants continue to enjoy the right to buy.

Calculating the qualifying period

The qualifying period is calculated in accordance with the general rules. Note that for the purpose of determining whether at any time a housing association tenant was a public sector tenant, the association shall be deemed to have been registered at that time, even if it only subsequently secures registration.

Who has the right to buy?

The general conditions and exemptions to the right to buy apply to housing associations (see Chapter 2). Some of the exemptions are particular to housing associations, so that tenants of certain associations are not entitled to exercise their right.

Covenants in conveyance or lease (National Parks, etc)

Where the dwelling is situated in a National Park, an area of outstanding natural beauty or a designated rural area, the associaion may, in addition to the usual restrictions, include with the Housing Corporation's consent a covenant to the effect that if the owner sells within ten years of purchase, the dwelling must first be offered to the association.

Financial arrangements

Where a tenant exercises the right to buy, a housing association has to meet its own administration and legal costs and any tax liabilities. Costs incurred by the association cannot be passed on to the tenant. The association must repay any Housing Association grant made in respect of the dwelling, although this may be reduced in some circumstances. It must also repay any mortgage on the property and must notify the Housing Corporation of any agreed sale (although consent is not required).

Housing associations outside the right to buy

Except in so far as the right to acquire arises under the Housing Act 1996, assured tenants and tenants protected by the Rent Acts do not qualify for the right to buy. Former secure tenants of local authorities, and of some other bodies, who may be housing association tenants (e.g. on a transfer of stock) have the preserved right to buy (see Chapter 8).

A detailed examination of the powers of housing associations to dispose of their property other than pursuant to the right to buy or acquire is outside the scope of this book. Tenants who do not have the right to buy may, however, be able to avail themselves of various other schemes. For example, housing association tenants may participate in a shared owner-ship scheme. Voluntary schemes vary between associations.

The power of registered housing associations to dispose of land is given by section 8 of the Housing Associations Act 1985. Corporation consent is required to any disposal, even if the association is de-registered (Housing Associations Act 1985, s 9). See also the powers of registered social landlords to dispose of land under section 8 of the Housing Act 1996.

By section 11 of the Housing Act 1996, any discount must be repaid under a covenant to be included in the conveyance or lease, which is a charge on the property. There are restrictions on disposal of houses in National Parks.

Associations excluded from right

Charity housing trusts and associations

If the landlord is a housing trust or association which is a charity within the meaning of the Charities Act 1960, the right to buy is exempted (HA 1985, Sched 5, para 2). "Housing trust" is defined in section 6 of HA 1985 as a corporation or body of persons which is required:

    1. to use the whole of its funds, including any surplus, to provide housing accommodation, or

    2. to devote its funds for charitable purposes and in fact uses them to provide housing accommodation.

Even where a trust is administered by a local authority (e.g. under the terms of a will) it remains a housing trust, and the tenants of property held under the trust do not have the right to buy (*London Borough of Hounslow v Hare et al* (1990) 24 HLR 9).

    "Housing association" is defined by section 5 of HA 1985 and essentially comprises any society, body of trustees or company which does not trade for profit and which has amongst its powers or objects, or were established for, certain housing purposes.

Co-operative housing associations

Co-operative housing association tenants are excluded from the right (HA 1985, Sched 5, para 2). These associations are defined in section 5(2) of HA 1985 as fully mutual housing associations which are societies registered under the Industrial and Provident Societies Act 1965. To be fully mutual an association's rules must restrict the membership to persons who are tenants or prospective tenants, and preclude the granting or assignment of tenancies to persons other than members.

No receipt of government funds

Even if not a charitable trust or association or a co-operative, secure tenants of housing associations which have at no time received one of the grants listed in paragraph 3 of Schedule 5 to HA 1985 are exempt from the right to buy. The relevant grants are those made under:

- Paragraph 2 of Schedule 1 to the Housing Associations Act 1985 (grants under enactments superseded by the Housing Act 1974
- Section 31 of the Housing Act 1974 (management grants)
- Section 41 of the Housing Associations Act 1985 (housing association grants)
- Section 54 of the Housing Associations Act 1985 (revenue deficit grants)
- Section 55 of the Housing Associations Act 1985 (hostel deficit grants)
- Section 58(2) of the Housing Associations Act 1985 (grants by local authorities)
- Section 50 of the Housing Act 1988 (housing associations grants)
- Section 51 of the Housing Act 1988 (revenue deficit grants).

This does not include renovation grants, but the first category does include basic residual subsidy received under the Housing Finance Act 1972 (*Wood v South Western Co-operative Housing Society* (1982) 4 HLR 101).

Leasehold schemes for the elderly

Leasehold schemes for the elderly can be promoted by charitable housing associations. Long leases may be granted by housing associations who house the elderly. A long lease may be granted to elderly persons or persons nominated by the landlord.

Tenants' incentive scheme

This scheme was introduced in April 1990 with a two-fold aim: first to free up housing association tenancies for letting to the homeless; and secondly to help housing association tenants purchase homes.

The scheme

The scheme has been revised at various times (see e.g Housing Corporation Circular 27/92). It is designed to make accommodation available for persons accepted by the local authority as statutorily homeless. Existing tenants are offered cash incentives to vacate their property and buy a home of their own on the open market. If a property, once vacant, is not used immediately to house a homeless person, it must be shown that another property was made available. There is no obligation on local authorities to nominate a person whom the association regard as suitable. Funding may be provided by the Housing Corporation and other sources. Incentives are also available for tenants whose families wish to extend their homes so that the tenant can move in with them.

Eligibility

The scheme is open to all registered housing associations which are allowed to participate under their own rules. Mutual co-operatives may participate but cannot use their own resources, and charitable housing associations must use wholly non-charitable sources.

Tenants do not have any legal right to claim the cash incentive, and may only participate in the scheme in accordance with the Corporation's published criteria. The legal provisions for the scheme relate only to the Corporation's power to pay grants under sections 50, 52 and 53 of the Housing Act 1988.

The tenant must have been a public sector tenant, as defined by the DoE, for at least two years (see the Tenant Incentive Scheme Procedure Guide). A tenant or joint tenant who already owns a residential property is not eligible, nor are employees of the association.

Procedure

The housing association is required to enter into a programme agreement with the Corporation. For the level of the cash incentive, see the Tenant Incentive Scheme Procedure Guide. The purchase must be approved by the association (certain properties, including properties abroad, cannot be purchased) and completion should take place within six months of approval.

Right to acquire under Housing Act 1996

The extension of the right to buy to all tenants of registered social landlords, including those whose secure tenants have neither the right to buy nor the preserved right to buy under previous legislation, is a further attempt to pursue the right to buy philosophy.

Under sections 16 and 17 of the Housing Act 1996, a tenant of a registered social landlord has, in certain circumstances, the right to acquire the dwelling of which he or she is a tenant.

Registered social landlord

The Corporation is required to maintain a register of social landlords under section 1. A body is eligible for registration under section 2 if it is:

1. a registered charity which is a housing association;
2. a society registered under the Industrial and

Provident Societies Act 1965 which satisfies the conditions in
sub-section (2); or

3. a company registered under the Companies Act
1985 which satisfies those conditions.

The conditions in section 2(2) are that the body is non-profit
making and is established for the purpose of, or has among
its objects or powers, the provision, construction, improvement or management of:

1. houses to be kept available for letting;
2. houses for occupation by members of the body,
where the rules of the body restrict membership to persons
entitled or prospectively entitled (as tenants or otherwise) to
occupy a house provided or managed by the body; or
3. hostels;

and that any additional purposes or objects are among those
specified in section 2(4).

There may in addition be other requirements for registration, imposed by the Secretary of State under section 5.

Who has the right to acquire?

To have the right to acquire the applicant must satisfy the
tenant qualification and the dwelling qualification. In addition the requirements of certain parts of the Housing Act
1985 right to buy provisions must also be satisfied.

The tenant qualification

He or she must be a tenant under an assured or secure tenancy. Tenants are excluded if they have an assured shorthold
tenancy or a long tenancy (as defined in sections 187 and 115
of HA 1985 – essentially any lease for a term certain of at
least 21 years). There is no provision for tenants with Rent
Act protection to have the right to acquire.

The dwelling qualification

The dwelling must have been provided with public money and have remained in the social rented sector. "Provided with public money" is defined in section 16(2) of the 1996 Act and means any of the following:

1. Provided or acquired wholly or in part by a grant under section 18 of the Housing Act 1996, and the Corporation, when making the grant, notified the recipient that the grant was to be made under section 18, allowing time for the applicant to withdraw. When a registered social landlord acquires property under section 18, it will be aware that any future tenant may have the right to acquire it.

2. Provided or acquired wholly or in part by applying or appropriating sums standing in the disposal proceeds fund of a registered social landlord under section 25 of the Housing Act 1996. (The disposal proceeds fund is the fund into which are paid monies from previous sales).

3. Acquired by a registered social landlord after the commencement of section 16(2) on a disposal by a public sector landlord at a time when it was capable of being let as a separate dwelling.

Tenants only have the right to acquire under the Housing Act 1996 if their dwelling was provided or acquired after the commencement of Chapter III of Part I of the Housing Act 1996.

"Remaining within the social rented sector" is defined in section 16(3) and means that both of the following criteria must be satisfied:

1. the person holding the freehold has been, at all times since it was provided or acquired, a registered social landlord or a public sector landlord; and

2. any lessee (but not a mortgagee) has been an individual (but not a long leaseholder) or a registered social landlord or a public sector landlord.

Application of Part V of HA 1985

The tenant must satisfy the provisions of Part V of HA 1985, but the Secretary of State has the general power to modify application of Part V by regulations, which will set out the amended text of Part V, made under section 17 of the 1996 Act. The regulations may be either general or specific to certain classes or areas.

The relevant regulations are The Housing (Right to Acquire) Regulations 1997 (SI 1997 No 619). The regulations exclude the right to buy on rent to mortgage terms and the preserved right to buy. While the exceptions to the right to buy in paras 1, 3 and 11 of Schedule 5 (charities; certain housing associations; certain dwelling-houses for the elderly) are lifted, three new exemptions are added: dwelling-houses in designated rural areas; dwelling-houses for persons with special needs and dwelling-houses charged with debts equal to or greater than the purchase price plus discount. The restrictions on the disposals in National Parks etc. are disapplied. Provisions are also added to Schedule 6 of the right to buy provisions on the discharge or release of charges on the landlord's interest in the dwelling-house.

Exemption

The Secretary of State has power to designate rural areas where the right to acquire will not apply (Housing Act 1996, s 17(1)(b)). A number of statutory instruments have been made for each area of the country: SI 1997 No 620 (West Midlands); SI 1997 No 621 (South West); SI 1997 No 622 (North West and Merseyside); SI 1997 No 623 (East); SI 1997 No 624 (North East); SI 1996 No 625 (South East); SI 1997 No 685, Wales. These set out those areas which are exempt.

Procedure and price

The right to acquire will operate as a modification of Part V of HA 1985. The Secretary of State has the specific power, however, to specify the rate of discount (Housing Act 1996, s 17(1)(a)). The Housing (Right to Acquire) (Discount) Order 1997 (SI 1997 No 626) sets out the discount in England, which is set at a fixed sum, ranging between £16,000 and £9,000 depending on the location of the dwelling-house. In Wales the discount is fixed by the Housing (Right to Acquire) (Discount) (Wales) Order 1997 (SI 1997 No 569) at 25 per cent of the open market value, subject to a maximum of £16,000.

Consultation

The Secretary of State must consult the local authorities or housing authorities before making changes which will affect applicants in their area, and "such bodies appearing to him to be representative of registered social landlords as he considers appropriate".

Voluntary sales

In addition to those who have the right to acquire (which only apply to new lettings after commencement of the Housing Act 1996), it is expected that a voluntary purchase scheme will also be introduced. A registered social landlord has the power, modelled on section 8 of the Housing Associations Act 1985, to dispose of land under section 8 of the 1996 Act. Charities may dispose of land without the constraints of section 39 of the Settled Land Act 1925, which identifies the conditions on which settled land can be sold, provided the disposal is within the charity's rules. The Corporation's consent is required under sections 9 and 12 of the Housing Associations Act 1985. A disposal without consent may in some circumstances be void. Certain lettings do not require consent.

Tenants of existing stock may qualify under a voluntary scheme, subject to the provisions of sections 11-15 of the 1996 Act.

Index

Acquisition under Housing Act 1996. *See* Right to acquire under Housing Act 1996

Agreement
superior lease, in, 91

Agricultural holding
dwelling-house as part of, not secure tenancy, 8

Aided school. *See* Governors of aided school

Almshouse charity
licence granted by, not secure tenancy, 8

Armed forces accommodation
qualifying period, 20-21

Block of flats
exception for, 33

Business
premises occupied for purposes of, not secure tenancy, 8

Care, duty of
landlord's offer notice, 41-42

Change in landlord's interest. *See* Landlords

Charge on property
priority of charges, 79-81
repayment of discount, 79-81

Charitable housing trust
landlord condition, 7

Charity
housing association which is, 23, 134
housing trust which is, 22, 134

Co-operative housing association
excepted landlord, as, 23, 134
landlord condition, 7, 22

Completion
changes in landlord's interest, 114
discovering loss after, 97-98
enforcement of, 104-105
failure to complete,
first notice to complete, 47-48
generally, 46-47
second notice to complete, 48-49
first notice to complete, 47-48
procedure, 43-44
rent to mortgage terms, acquisition on, 70
second notice to complete, 48-49
status of other occupiers on, 44

Consultation
right to acquire under Housing Act 1996, relating to, 140

Conveyance. *See* Grant or conveyance

Cost floor
percentage entitlement, 61

Costs
landlord, of, 37-38
rent to mortgage terms, calculation of, 91
redemption, costs of, 74
valuation, 73-74

Covenants
extended right to buy, 130
freehold conveyance, included in, 83-84
grant of lease, included in, landlord, by, 84-86

nature of interest, 84
rights to be included, 84
tenant, by, 86-91
leasehold and freehold
interests, common to,
other covenants and
conditions, 82-83
related rights, 81-82
restrictive covenants, 82
rights to be conveyed or
granted, 81
National Parks, 132
related rights, 81-82
restrictive, 82
rights to be conveyed or
granted, 81
Crown tenant
exception to right to buy, 23
Curtilage
building within, 23-24

Death of tenant
loss of right to buy, 95
widow(er)'s right to buy, 17-18
Declaration
enforcing completion, 104-105
intermediate stages, 103-104
Delays
extension of time,
mandatory, 46
voluntary, 46
landlord, by,
counter notice (form RTB 7),
50-51
generally, 49
initial notice of delay (form
RTB 6), 49-50
loss of right to buy, 97
operative notice of delay
(form RTB 8), 51-52
rent to mortgage terms,
acquisition on, 71

notice of delay,
counter notice (form RTB 7),
50-51
initial (form RTB 6),
49-50
operative (form RTB 8),
51-52
reduction for operative
notice of delay, 57
procedural, dealing with,
45-52
rent to mortgage terms,
acquisition on, 70-71
tenant, by,
failure to complete, 46-49
notice of intention, failure
to serve, 45-46
rent to mortgage terms,
acquisition on, 70-71
Determination. See Disputes
about valuation
Development Board for Rural
Wales
employment-related
tenancy, 9
landlord condition, 7, 21-22
preserved rights, 117
Development land
dwelling-house on, not
secure tenancy, 7
Disabled tenant
dwelling-house for, 25-26
Discount
amount of, 60
change of tenant, 63
entitlement to,
generally, 60, 61-62
previous purchasers, 62
percentage entitlement,
amount of, 60-61
cost floor, 61
maximum discount, 61

repayment of,
   amount to be repaid, 78-79
   calculating three-year
     period, 79
   charge on property, 79-81
   exempt disposals, 78
   extended right to buy, 129
   generally, 76-77
   relevant disposals, 77
   rent to mortgage, 78-79
Disposal of landlord's interest.
   See Preservation of right to
   buy
Disputes about valuation
   determination,
     final, 58
     generally, 58
     procedure following, 59-60
   district valuer,
     challenging, 59
     procedure by, 59
   generally, 57-58
   re-determination, 58
   See also Enforcement
District valuer
   challenging, 59
   procedure by, 59
Division of dwelling-house
   horizontal, 31
   vertical, 31-32
Duty of care. *See* Care, duty of
Dwelling-house
   disabled tenant, for,
     mentally disabled, 26
     physically disabled, 25-26
   division of,
     horizontal, 31
     vertical, 31-32
   elderly tenant, for, 26-28
   flat, meaning, 30
   horizontal division, 31
   house, meaning, 30

Housing Act 1996, right to
   acquire under, 139
interest to be conveyed or
   granted,
     blocks of flats, exception
      for, 33
     freehold, 33
     length of lease, 33
land treated as included in,
   29-30, 130
material part over remainder
   of structure, 32
purchase of, 29-30
reasonableness test, 31
right to acquire under
   Housing Act 1996, 139
value of,
     assumptions, 54-57
     conduct of valuation, 53-54
     generally, 53
vertical division, 31-32

Educational course
   accommodation relating to,
     not secure tenancy, 8
Elderly tenants
   dwelling-house for, 26-28
   leasehold schemes for, 135
Employment-related tenancy
   excepted property, as, 23-25
   not secure tenancy, 7, 9-10
Enforcement
   completion, of, 104-105
   financial assistance, 110-111
   generally, 103
   injunctions and declarations,
     enforcing completion,
      104-105
     intermediate stages,
      103-104
   intervention of Secretary of
     State,

direct, 107-110
    financial assistance, 110-111
judicial review, 106-107
maladministration, allegation
    of, 103
Exceptions to right to buy
    disabled tenant, dwelling-
        house for,
            mentally disabled tenant,
                26
            physically disabled
                tenant, 25-26
    elderly tenant, dwelling-
        house for, 26-28
    employment-related tenancy,
        23-25
    excepted landlord, 22-23
    excepted property,
        disabled tenant, dwelling-
            house for, 25-26
        elderly tenant, dwelling-
            house for, 26-28
        employment-related
            tenancy, 23-25
    generally, 22
    insufficient interest in
        property, 23
    mentally disabled tenant, 26
    physically disabled tenant,
        25-26
    property,
        excepted, 23-28
        insufficient interest in, 23
    void prohibition or
        restriction, 22
Exercising right to buy. See
    Procedure
Extended right to buy
    application of, 122
    assistance to freeholder, 129
    covenants in conveyance, 130
    discount, repayment of, 129

generally, 121
land, inclusion of, 130
legislation, 121-122
modifications of right to buy,
    122-123
preservation of, 120
procedure,
    admitting right, 123
    apportionment of purchase
        price, 125
    change of landlord or
        tenant, 124-125
    claiming right to buy, 123
    denying right, 123
    execution of conveyance,
        125
    notice of offer, 124
    withdrawal of tenant's
        right, 123-124
registration of title, 128
rent to mortgage terms,
    acquisition on,
        admitting right, 126
        apportionment of initial
            payment, 127
        change of landlord, 127
        claiming right, 126
        denying right, 126
        execution of conveyance,
            127-128
        redemption of freeholder's
            share, 128
        withdrawal of notice,
            126-127
repayment of discount, 129
Secretary of State's power to
    intervene, 129
tenant's notice (form RTB 1),
    38, 123-124
tenant's notice of delay,
    128
title, registration of, 128

Extension of time
  mandatory, 46
  voluntary, 46

Family members
  meaning, 14-15
  right to buy, 13-14
  section 122 notice, service of,
    13, 15
  tenant's notice (form RTB 1),
    38
Finance
  housing association,
    arrangements of, 132-133,
    135
  intervention of Secretary of
    State, 110-111
Fire authority
  accommodation provided by,
    not secure tenancy, 10
Flat
  blocks of flats, exception for,
    33
  insufficient interest in, 23
  interest to be conveyed or
    granted, 33
  length of lease, 33
  material part over remainder
    of structure, 32
  meaning, 30
Freehold
  assistance to freeholder, 129
  conveyance. *See* Grant or
    conveyance
  covenants. *See* Covenants
  tenant's basic entitlement to, 29

Government funds
  no receipt of, 135
Governors of aided school
  employment-related tenancy,
    9, 25

Grant or conveyance
  covenants,
    common to leasehold and
      freehold interests, 81-83
    extended right to buy, 130
    freehold conveyance,
      included in, 83-84
    grant of lease, included in,
      84-91
    landlord, by, 84-86
    National Parks, 132
    restrictive, 82
    tenant, by, 86-91
  execution of conveyance, 125,
    127-128
  future disposals,
    agreement in superior
      lease, 91
    tenants in National Parks,
      by, 91-92
  generally, 76
  rent to mortgage terms,
    acquisition on,
      compulsory redemption
        of landlord's share,
        72-73
      costs of redemption, 74
      generally, 72
      other covenants, 74
      valuation costs, 73-74
  repayment of discount,
    amount to be repaid, 78-79
    charge on property, 79-81
    exempt disposals, 78
    generally, 76-77
    relevant disposals, 77
    rent to mortgage, 78-79
  restrictive covenants, 82
  terms in,
    rent to mortgage terms,
      acquisition on, 72-74
    valuation assumptions, 57

High Court
  service of notices, 35
Homelessness
  temporary accommodation,
    not secure tenancy, 7
Homosexual relationship
  family member, meaning, 14
Horizontal division
  divided, meaning, 31
  dwelling-house, purchase of,
    31
House
  interest to be conveyed or
    granted, 33
  length of lease, 33
  material part over remainder
    of structure, 32
  meaning, 30
Housing Act 1996. *See* Right to
  acquire under Housing Act
  1996
Housing action trust
  employment-related tenancy,
    9, 25
  landlord condition, 7, 21
Housing association
  charitable, 23, 134
  co-operative. *See* Co-operative
    housing association
  excepted landlord, as, 23, 131
  financial arrangements,
    132-133
  meaning, 134
  outside right to buy, 133-135
  within right to buy, 132-133
Housing benefit
  entitlement to, 65
Housing co-operative. *See*
  Co-operative housing
  association
Housing Corporation
  landlord condition, 7, 22

Housing for Wales
  landlord condition, 22
Housing trust
  charitable, 22, 134
  excepted landlord, as, 22-23
  meaning, 134
  See also Housing action trust
Husband and wife
  family member, meaning,
    14-15
  See also Spouse

Improvements
  contributions, 56, 90
  covenants by tenant, 87
  disregard of, 55-56
  See also Repairs and
    maintenance
Income
  rent to mortgage terms, right
    to acquire on, 65-67
Ineligibility for right to buy
  circumstances of, 98
  Insolvency Act proceedings,
    100
  possession order,
    generally, 98-99
    joint tenants, 99
    timing of order, 99-100
Injunction
  enforcing completion,
    104-105
  intermediate stages, 103-104
Insolvency
  ineligibility for right to buy,
    100
Insurance
  normal risks, 87
Internal repairs
  covenants by tenant, 86
  disregard of disrepair,
    55-56

Joint tenants
  ineligibility for right to buy, 99
  loss of right by, 12-13, 94
  periodic tenancy, 12
  right to buy, 12-13
Judicial review
  application for, 106-107

Land
  dwelling-house, treated as
    included in, 29-30, 130
Landlords
  acceptance (form RTB 2), 39
  change in interest of,
    completion already taken
      place, 114
    generally, 112
    preservation of right to
      buy, 114-120
    right to buy admitted,
      112-113
    right to buy already
      denied, 113-114
  change of, 71-72, 124-125, 127
  costs, 37-38
  covenants to repair and
    maintain,
      exclusion of, 85-86
      generally, 84-85
      leaseholder, landlord as,
        85
  delay by,
    counter notice (form RTB
      7), 50-51
    generally, 49
    initial notice of delay (form
      RTB 6), 49-50
    loss of right to buy, 97
    operative notice of delay
      (form RTB 8), 51-52
    rent to mortgage terms,
      acquisition on, 71

denial (form RTB 2), 39
disposal of interest. See
  Preservation of right to buy
excepted, 22-23
offer notice,
  contents, 40-41
  duty of care, 41-42
  service of, 39-40
  structural defect, 41
place of service, 35-36
qualifying period, condition
  for, 21-22
rent to mortgage terms. See
  Rent to mortgage terms
reply to tenant's notice,
  acceptance or denial (form
    RTB 2), 39
  generally, 38-39
  offer notice, 39-42
secure tenancy, requirements
  of, 6-7
superior, 87
withdrawal by, 102-103
Lease
  grant of. See Grant or
    conveyance
  length of, 33
  short-term arrangements, not
    secure tenancy, 8, 10
  superior, agreement in, 91
Leasehold
  covenants. See Covenants
  elderly, schemes for, 135
  tenant's basic entitlement to,
    29
Licensed premises
  dwelling-house consisting of,
    not secure tenancy, 8
Local authority
  employment-related tenancy,
    9, 25
  landlord condition, 6, 21, 22

preserved rights, 116
Long tenancy
    not secure tenancy, 7
Loss of right to buy
    change of tenant, 101-102
    circumstances where right
        may be lost,
            generally, 93
            ineligibility for right to
                buy, 98-100
            security, loss of, 93-98
    generally, 93
    ineligibility for right to buy,
        generally, 98
        Insolvency Act proceedings,
            100
        possession order, 98-100
    joint tenant, by, 12-13, 94
    lapse of right to buy, 102-103
    rent to mortgage terms, right
        to acquire on, 64-65
    security, loss of,
        death of tenant, 95
        discovering loss after
            completion, 97-98
        generally, 93
        joint tenants, 94
        only or principal home, 94
        subletting, 94
        timing of, 95-97
    tenant,
        change of, 101-102
        deemed withdrawal by,
            102
        withdrawal by, 102
    withdrawal,
        deemed, 102
        landlord, by, 102-103
        tenant, by, 102

Maintenance. See Repairs and
    maintenance

Marriage
    family member, meaning,
        15
    previous, of deceased spouse,
        19
Material part over remainder of
    structure
        meaning, 32
Matrimonial home
    joint tenant, effect of property
        transfer order on, 12
    parent's home, acquiring
        tenancy of, 20
    tenant condition, 6
Mentally disabled tenant
    dwelling-house for, 26
Mistakes
    notices, in, 36
Mortgage. See Rent to mortgage
    terms

National Parks
    covenants in conveyance or
        lease, 132
    preserved rights, 117
    tenants in, limitations on
        future disposals by,
            91-92
New town corporation
    employment-related tenancy,
        9, 25
    landlord condition, 6, 21, 22
Northern Ireland
    landlord condition, 22
Notices
    counter notice (form RTB 7),
        50-51
    landlord's offer notice,
        contents, 40-41
        duty of care, 41-42
        service of, 39-40
        structural defect, 41

mistakes in, 36
notice of delay,
    counter notice (form RTB 7),
      50-51
    initial (form RTB 6), 49-50
    operative (form RTB 8),
      51-52
    reduction for operative
      notice of delay, 57
service of,
    method of, 35
    place of, 35-36
tenant's notice (form RTB 1),
    extended right to buy, 38,
      123-124
    family members, 38
    landlord's reply to, 38-42
    service of, 38
    withdrawal of, 123-124
tenant's notice of intention,
    failure to serve, 45-46
    proceeding with claim,
      42
    rent to mortgage terms,
      acquisition on, 69
    seeking rent to mortgage
      terms, 43
    service of, 42
    withdrawing claim, 43

Occupation
    completion, status of other
      occupiers on, 44
    family members, requirements
      relating to, 15
    order, effect on joint tenant,
      12
Ombudsman
    maladministration, complaint
      relating to, 103
Ouster injunction
    joint tenant, effect on, 12

Parent
    home of, acquiring tenancy
      of, 20
Percentage entitlement. *See*
    Discount
Periodic tenancy
    joint tenant, service of notice
      to quit by, 12
Physically disabled tenant
    dwelling-house for, 25-26
Place of service
    landlord, 35-36
    tenant, 36
Police authority
    accommodation provided by,
      not secure tenancy, 10
Possession
    action, conflict with enforcing
      completion, 104-105
    order for, ineligibility for
      right to buy, 98-100
    vacant, 57
Preservation of right to buy
    disposal of landlord's
      interest,
        further, 119-120
        generally, 118
        new landlord, landlord
          condition satisfied by,
          119
        part disposal, 119-120
        termination of landlord's
          interest, 120
        unregistered preserved
          right, 119
    exceptions to preserved right,
      115
    extended right to buy, 120
    generally, 114-115
    moves by tenant, 117-118
    preserved rights,
      generally, 116

main modifications, 116-117
qualifying person,
    modifications to reflect,
    116
qualification of preserved
    right, 115
qualifying persons, 115
tenant, moves by, 117-118
unregistered preserved right,
    119
Price
amount tenant has to pay, 53
apportionment of, 125
discount,
    change of tenant, 63
    entitlement to, 60, 61-62
    percentage entitlement,
        60-61
disputes about valuation,
    challenging district valuer,
        59
    determination, 58
    generally, 57-58
    procedure by district
        valuer, 59
    procedure following
        determination, 59-60
    re-determination, 58
Housing Act 1996, right to
    acquire under, 140
paying for property, 63
rent to mortgage terms. See
    Rent to mortgage terms
right to acquire under
    Housing Act 1996, 140
valuation of dwelling-house,
    assumptions, 54-57
    conduct of, 53-54
    disputes about, 57-60
    generally, 53
    operative notice of delay,
        reduction for, 57

Procedure
basic, 37
completion,
    generally, 43
    status of other occupiers
        on, 44
delay,
    dealing with, 45-52
    landlord, by, 49-52
    tenant, by, 45-49
extended right to buy. See
    Extended right to buy
generally, 34
Housing Act 1996, right to
    acquire under, 140
landlord,
    acceptance or denial (form
        RTB 2), 39
    costs of, 37-38
    delay by, 49-52
    offer notice, 39-42
    place of service, 35-36
    reply of, 38-42
mistakes in notices, 36
notices,
    mistakes in, 36
    service of, 35-36
    tenant, of, (form RTB 1), 38
registration of title, 44-45
right to acquire under
    Housing Act 1996, 140
service of notices,
    High Court practice, 35
    method of, 35
    place of service, 35-36
tenant,
    delay by, 45-49
    notice (form RTB 1), 38
    notice of intention, 42-43
    place of service, 36
tenants' incentive scheme, 137
title, registration of, 44-45

Property
  charge on,
    generally, 79
    priority of charges, 79-81
  excepted,
    disabled tenant, dwelling-
      house for, 25-26
    elderly tenant, dwelling-
      house for, 26-28
    employment-related
      tenancy, 23-25
    insufficient interest in, 23
    paying for, 63
Property transfer order
  joint tenant, effect on, 12
Public body
  employment, tenancy
    connected with, 9
Public sector tenant
  landlord condition for
    qualifying period, 21-22
  meaning, 21
  previous spouse as, 19
  secure tenant as, 17
  spouse as, 18
Purchase price. *See* Price
Purchaser
  previous, entitlement to
    discount, 62

Qualifying period
  armed forces accommodation,
    20-21
  deceased spouse's previous
    marriage, 19
  deceased tenant,
    widower(er)'s right to buy,
    17-18
  parent's home, acquiring
    tenancy of, 20
  previous spouse was public
    sector tenant, 19

public sector tenant,
  landlord condition, 21-22
  meaning, 21
  previous spouse was, 19
  spouse is, 18
relevant periods,
  armed forces
    accommodation, 20-21
  deceased spouse's previous
    marriage, 19
  deceased tenant,
    widower(er)'s right to
    buy, 17-18
  parent's home, acquiring
    tenancy of, 20
  previous spouse was public
    sector tenant, 19
  reserved periods, 21
  secure tenant and spouse,
    17
  secure tenant, 17
  spouse is public sector
    tenant, 18
  widower(er)'s right to buy,
    17-18
reserved periods, 21
secure tenant,
  generally, 17
  spouse, and, 17
spouse,
  deceased, previous
    marriage of, 19
  previous, as public sector
    tenant, 19
  public sector tenant, as, 18
  secure tenant and, 17
two-year, 16

Reasonableness test
  dwelling-house, meaning, 31
Registered housing association
  landlord condition, 7

Registered social landlord
  eligibility for registration,
    137-138
  landlord condition, 22
  requirements relating to,
    137-138
Registration of title
  extended right to buy, 128
  procedure, 44-45
Rent to mortgage terms
  costs,
    calculation of, 91
    redemption, of, 74
    valuation, 73-74
  discount, repayment of, 78-79
  extension of right. *See*
    Extended right to buy
  housing benefit, entitlement
    to, 65
  income too high,
    generally, 65
    maximum initial payment,
      66
    minimum initial payment,
      66-67
  initial payment,
    maximum, 66
    minimum, 66-67
  landlord,
    change of, 71-72
    compulsory redemption of
      share, 72-73
    delay by, 71
    redemption of share, 74-75
    reply of, 67-69
  loss of right to buy, 64-65
  persons entitled to scheme,
    64
  preserved rights, 116
  procedure,
    change of landlord, 71-72
    claim, 67

    completion, 70
    delay, dealing with, 70-71
    landlord's reply, 67-69
    notice of terms, 69-70
    tenant's notice of intention,
      69
    withdrawal, 71
  redemption,
    costs of, 74
    landlord's share, of, 74-75
  repayment of discount, 78-79
  right to acquire on, 43, 63-75
  tenant,
    delay by, 70-71
    notice of intention, 69
  terms in conveyance or grant,
    compulsory redemption of
      landlord's share, 72-73
    costs of redemption, 74
    generally, 72
    other covenants, 74
    valuation costs, 73-74
  when right cannot be exercised,
    housing benefit, entitlement
      to, 65
    income too high, 65-67
    loss of right to buy, 64-65
Repairs and maintenance
  internal disrepair, disregard
    of, 55-56
  itemised works of repair, 89
  landlord, covenants by,
    exclusion of, 85-86
    generally, 84-85
    leaseholder, landlord as,
      85
  non-itemised works of repair,
    89
  tenant, covenants by,
    internal repairs, 86
    service charges and other
      contributions, 86-91

Repayment of discount. *See* Discount

Restrictive covenants
  nature of, 82

Right to acquire under Housing Act 1996
  application of Part V of HA 1985, 140
  consultation, 140-141
  dwelling qualification, 139
  exemption, 140
  extension of right to buy, 137
  generally, 137
  price, 140
  procedure, 140
  registered social landlord, 137-138
  tenant qualification, 138
  who has right to buy, 138-140

Right to buy
  enforcement. *See* Enforcement
  extended. *See* Extended right to buy
  family members. *See* Family members
  joint tenants. *See* Joint tenants
  loss of. *See* Loss of right to buy
  preservation of. *See* Preservation of right to buy
  secure tenancy. *See* Secure tenancy
  exceptions

Sales
  voluntary, 141

School
  aided. *See* Governors of aided school

Scotland
  landlord condition, 22

Scottish Homes
  landlord condition, 22

Secretary of State
  intervention of,
    direct, 107-110
    extended right to buy, relating to, 129
    financial assistance, 110-111
  prescribed bodies, 22

Section 122 notice
  family members, relating to, 13, 15

Secure tenancy
  extension of right. *See* Extended right to buy
  family members, right to buy of, 13-15
  joint tenancy, 12-13
  loss of security, 10-11, 93-98
  qualifying period. *See* Qualifying period
  requirements of,
    five conditions, 5-6
    landlord condition, 6-7
    tenant condition, 6
  right to buy, 5
  tenancy not secure, 7-10

Service charges
  covenants by tenant, 86-91
  initial period,
    limitations in, 87-89
    nature of, 90
  valuation assumptions, 56

Service of notices
  High Court Practice, 35
  method of, 35
  place of,
    landlord, 35-36
    tenant, 36

Short-term lease arrangements
  not secure tenancy, 8, 10

Social landlord. *See* Registered
   social landlord
Spouse
   deceased, previous marriage
      of, 19
   previous, as public sector
      tenant, 19
   public sector tenant, as, 18
   secure tenant and, 17
Structural defect
   meaning, 41
Subletting
   loss of security, 93
Superior lease
   agreement in, 91

Temporary accommodation
   not secure tenancy, 7-8
Tenancy
   employment-related. *See*
      Employment-related tenancy
   secure. *See* Secure tenancy
Tenants
   change of, 101-102, 124-125
   deemed withdrawal by, 102
   delay by,
      failure to complete, 46-49
      failure to serve notice of
         intention, 45-46
      rent to mortgage terms,
         acquisition on, 70-71
   elderly, 26-28, 135
   extension of right. *See*
      Extended right to buy
   Housing Act 1996, right to
      acquire under, 138
   joint,
      loss of right by, 12-13, 94
      right to buy, 12-13
   moves by, 117-118
   National Parks, in, limitations
      on future disposals by, 91-92

notice (form RTB 1),
   extended right to buy, 38,
      123-124
   family members, 38
   landlord's reply to, 38-42
   service of, 38
   withdrawal of, 123-124
notice of intention,
   failure to serve, 45-46
   proceeding with claim, 42
   rent to mortgage terms,
      acquisition on, 69
   seeking rent to mortgage
      terms, 43
   service of, 42
   withdrawing claim, 43
place of service, 36
public sector. *See* Public
   sector tenant
rent to mortgage terms. *See*
   Rent to mortgage terms
right to acquire under
   Housing Act 1996, 138
withdrawal by, 102
Tenants' incentive scheme
   eligibility, 136-137
   introduction of, 136
   nature of, 136
   procedure, 137
Title
   registration of, 44-45, 128

Urban development
   corporation
      employment-related
         tenancy, 9, 25
      landlord condition, 7, 21

Vacant possession
   valuation assumptions, 57
Valuation
   assumptions, 54-57

disputes about,
  challenging district valuer,
    59
  determination, 58
  generally, 57-58
  procedure by district
    valuer, 59
  procedure following
    determination, 59-60
  re-determination, 58
dwelling-house, of, 53-57
improvement contributions,
  56
improvements, disregard of,
  55-56
internal disrepair, disregard
  of, 55-56
no existing interest in
  purchase, 57

operative notice of delay,
  reduction for, 57
service charges, 56
terms of grant or conveyance,
  57
vacant possession, 57
who should conduct, 53-54
Vertical division
  dwelling-house, division of,
    31-32
Voluntary sales
  introduction of, 141

Widow(er)
  right to buy of, 17-18
Works
  dwelling-house available
    during, not secure tenancy,
    8

OTHER BOOKS AVAILABLE IN ARDEN'S HOUSING LIBRARY

Compulsory Competitive Tendering of Housing Management

Law and practice in the management of social housing

Caroline Hunter and Andy Selman

Clearly setting out the legal framework, this book goes through each step in contracting the service from first drafts, through advertising and letting, to monitoring and re-specifying. The organisation of in-house bids get special attention, while the background and possible future direction of CCT are not forgotten.

Here to help local authorities through the process, this guide offers invaluable support to staff letting and monitoring the contracts. But it also provides essential information for the tenants whose views must be taken into account, the workforce whose jobs are at stake, and the councillors who are ultimately responsible for the contracts let. For any housing department trying to make CCT work to the best advantage, this is the book.

Arden's Housing Library vol.7

Paperback   176 pp   216 x 138mm   ISBN 1-898001-05-7

Dealing with Disrepair

A guide to inspection and diagnosis

Patrick Reddin, FRICS, FBEng

"The technical information is simply and clearly presented with useful building diagrams...its methodical approach will make it particularly useful as a training tool for both landlord and tenant." *Housing Agenda*

"...a valuable contribution to raising standards and customer care, efficiency and effectiveness..."

Royal Institution of Chartered Surveyors' president

Understanding buildings is something which is usually left up to surveyors. It shouldn't be. Millions of people suffer as a result of serious disrepair in their home. To remedy this quickly, housing managers need to understand the buildings their tenants are living in, accurately define what repair is needed and know how to get work done. This guide breaks new ground. It includes over 30 detailed cross-section drawings and good practice checklists.

Arden's Housing Library vol.6
Paperback   232 pp   216 x 138mm   illustrated
ISBN 1-898001-06-5

Repairs and Maintenance

Law and practice in the management of social housing

Alyson Kilpatrick, Barrister

"...an admirably concise but thorough exposition of the principles of the law in this area. The author, while impartial, is realistic about the problems faced by social landlords and practical in her advice..." *Housing Agenda*

Disrepair in Britain's ageing social housing stock is already a problem – and it's getting worse. Shortage of money often leaves landlords unable to attend to repairs. But not doing repairs can be even more costly – as buildings deteriorate further and tenants, denied the comfort and security of their homes, go to court.

This book provides landlords with a practical understanding of their own legal obligations and those of their tenants. Covering problem areas like condensation, this guide follows the process through, looking at the landlord's powers to get work done, and the role of housing staff when all else fails and court proceedings begin.

Contents include:

Social Landlord's Contractual Liabilities • Common Types of Complaint
• Tenants' Remedies • Public Health Duties • Tenants' Contractual Obligations
• Getting the Works Done • Improvements • Court Proceedings
• Compendium of Damages Awards • Sample Legal Pleadings
• Best Practice Checklists

Arden's Housing Library vol.5
Paperback   240pp   216 x 138mm   ISBN 1-898001-11-1

Presenting Possession Proceedings

Law and practice in the management of social housing

Andrew Dymond, Barrister

"Housing managers and officers involved in regaining possession should find this book invaluable." *ADC Review*

It can be unpleasant. It is certainly not easy but it has to be done. Sooner or later every social landlord is faced with taking back possession of a tenant's home when rent arrears have run out of control, when nuisance has become intolerable or when the tenant has disappeared leaving friends or relatives in residence.

With pressure to maximise rent income and minimise management costs, more and more housing managers and officers are going to find themselves handling the ensuing possession proceedings. Checklists are included to make sure proceedings will not run into the sand because of error or omission.

Contents include:

Commencing Possession Proceedings • What Needs to be Proved? • The Return Date • Pre-Trial Procedure • Evidence • The Trial • Rent Arrears Cases • Other Types of Possession Action • Possession Orders • Further Action • Court Forms

Arden's Housing Library vol.4
Paperback   200pp   216 x 138mm   ISBN 1-898001-15-4

Nuisance and Harassement

Law and practice in the management of social housing
Susan Belgrave, Barrister

"The guide is excellent." *Housing*

"I can see this book on many desks, somewhat battered and heavily thumbed." *Voluntary Housing*

Nuisance from neighbours is a vexed and growing problem, while the rise in cases of harassment is causing alarm. But action can be taken now against those guilty of causing nuisance. Local authorities are able to prosecute perpetrators of harassment. Race is one of the many reasons why people become the target of harassment, while cockroaches and traffic noise can be as much of a nuisance as other people's behaviour.

Contents include:
Laws Against Nuisance • Investigations and Alternatives to Litigation • Litigation • Laws Against Harassment • Practice and Procedures in Harassment Cases

Arden's Housing Library vol.3
Paperback   144pp   216 x 138mm   ISBN 1-898001-14-6

Tenants' Rights
Law and practice in the management of social housing
Caroline Hunter, Nottingham University

"Caroline Hunter has written very clearly and concisely and made extremely good use of case law, which is presented in a way that brings the text alive." *The Adviser*

Tenants' rights are a new area of law. Beginning in 1980, these rights have been swiftly developed and expanded. Secure tenants of councils and housing associations now have more control over their homes than ever before. So keeping abreast of tenants' rights is now essential for anyone working in the housing field – and this book is the way to do it.

As individuals, many tenants may now take in lodgers, exchange their homes or even sublet them. Often other family members can succeed to a tenancy. Collectively family members have new rights to information, to manage their own homes and even to change their landlord.

Contents include:
Historical background • Succession • Assignment, Lodgers and Subletting • Changing the Terms of the Tenancy • Information and Consultation • The Right to Manage • Estate Redevelopment

Arden's Housing Library vol.2
Paperback   136pp   216 x 138mm   ISBN 1-898001-13-8

Security of Tenure

Law and practice in the management of social housing

Andrew Dymond, Barrister

"readable . . . up-to-date, it includes well chosen examples and a helpful appendix." *The Adviser*

All housing managers know their way around the law on security of tenure. Or do they? What are the conditions that have to be met to make a tenancy secure? Exactly what steps should be taken before starting proceedings against tenants who are in arrears with rent? For experienced practitioners, this book is that indispensable companion which will always provide guidance in moments of doubt. For those approaching the subject for the first time, it is an invaluable summary of the law.

Contents include:

Status of the Occupier • Tenant or Licensee? • Secure and Assured Tenancies • Conditions for Security of Tenure • Seeking Possession • Grounds for Possession Against Secure Tenants • Grounds for Possession Against Assured Tenants • Suitable Alternative Accommodation • Reasonableness • Other Occupiers • Possession Orders • Termination by the Tenant

Arden's Housing Library vol.1
Paperback   172pp   216 x 138mm   ISBN 1-898001-12-X